Leave Me A Lawn

Lawn Care for Tired Gardeners

The Dreer Lawn Mower

Easy-Growing Gardening Guide, Vol. 7

Rosefiend Cordell

Rosefiend Publishing

ISBN: 978-1-953196-21-7

DEDICATION

To my father-in-law, Richard R. Cordell, who probably could have written this book himself. I'm pretty sure he'd rather farm than write. To be honest, I don't blame him one bit.

CONTENTS

ALL THE BOOKS I'VE WRITTEN SO FAR

The Easy-Growing Gardening Series
Don't Throw in the Trowel: Vegetable Gardening Month by Month
Rose to the Occasion: An Easy-Growing Guide to Rose Gardening
If You're a Tomato, I'll Ketchup With You: Tomato Gardening Tips and Tricks
Perennial Classics: Planting and Growing Great Perennial Gardens
Petal to the Metal: Growing Gorgeous Houseplants
Gardening Month by Month: Tips for Great Flowers, Vegetables, & Houseplants
Leave Me A Lawn: Lawn Care for Tired Gardeners
Japanese Beetles and Grubs: Trap, Spray, Control Them
Stay Grounded: Soil Building for Sustainable Gardens
Genius Gardening Hacks: Tips and Fixes for the Creative Gardener
Design of the Times: How to Plan Glorious Landscapes and Gardens

Civil War Books
Courageous Women of the Civil War: Soldiers, Spies, Medics, and More (Chicago Review Press, 2016)
Gentlemen, Accept This Facial Hair Challenge! Epic Beards and Moustaches of the Civil War

The Dragonriders of Skala series (written with Pauline Creeden)
The Flame of Battle
A Fire of Roses
A Crown of Flames
A Whisper of Smoke (a stand-alone prequel)

Young Adult Novels
Angel in the Whirlwind
Butterfly Chaos
Those Black Wings
Why Can't My Life Be a Romance Novel? A goofy romantic short
Fifteen Inches Tall and Bulletproof: Ten Short Stories

The White Oak Chronicles:
    The Chieftain (a stand-alone prequel)
    Outlander's Scar
    Wandering Stars
    Silverlady Descends

INTRODUCTION

A good-looking lawn can be a jewel in the landscape, while serving many different purposes to the homeowner: as a place around the house that's (generally) free of ticks and biting insects, to show off the house in the landscape, and to give kids a place to play and grownups a place to relax.

I don't remember much from my Turfgrass Management class, but I did learn something very valuable in that class. Dr. Fairchild said, "Nature hates a monoculture." If you get a big area filled with the same kind of plant, it's more likely to get attacked by insects and diseases. After all, if you were a hungry bug looking for a place to eat, would you go around hunting for a lone blade of grass standing among a sea of other plants, or would you land at the all-you-can-eat buffet that is somebody's luscious green lawn?

These words are very true, wherever you go in horticulture. And this is one of the reasons why lawns can be a challenge.

Nature prefers a variety – a mix – a diversity of plants. If you look at any place that's gone wild, you'll generally see many different species and kinds of plants growing in one spot – and, often, there's a certain group of species depending on how long this area has been left alone. So you'll start with a number of small mixed weeds like dandelions, crabgrass, and clover. And then larger plants come in, such as ragweed, pigweed, and small trees, usually mulberries or some other variety of "weed" tree, which are fast-growing trees that spread a lot. Then your slower-growing trees eventually catch up and take over and shade out the other smaller weed trees. Over 40 years, a wild area can turn into the beginnings of a nice forest. Anyway, this is called succession, as one group of plants is followed by another group of plants. But it's always a wide group of species, depending on location, climate, and thousands of other factors. And this succession always involves a variety of plants.

So basically, when you plant a lawn with a bunch of the same kinds of grass over a large area, nature's going to try and shake up the mix. Weed seeds drift in, and up pops a dandelion. Or a buttercup seed that gets brought to the surface while the ground is being harrowed germinates and raises a happy yellow cup among your fescue. Or the roots of a white clover plant, which survived the initial blast of Round-Up and tilling, starts growing and regenerates new clover plants. It happens a thousand different ways. That's just how nature works. So then you have to go spot-treating broadleaved plants (if you are an organic gardener) or start spraying broadleaf herbicide (if you are not organic).

Now, at my own house, my lawn is nothing to write home about. I have chickens and a dog and a cat and several yard rabbits and squirrels and occasionally a possum, so I let the yard go natural, and I never spray or put down Weed and Feed.

In fact, instead of nurturing the grass in my backyard, I keep throwing white clover seed out there simply because I like white clover and the scent of its flowers in June, especially when heat lays heavy over the ground, and then the scent is wonderful. The chickens like to eat the clover blossoms, and when the blossoms are finished, they eat the clover leaves. The clover plants fix nitrogen into the soil (that is, they take nitrogen from the air and put it in the ground, making it available for other plants), so that's good for the world underneath the soil. It's just what I prefer.

Obviously, letting your lawn grow random stuff is not an option for a lot of people. Some of you have to put up with homeowner's associations. Some of you come home at night from work and you're tired as heck and not up to weed and feeding the world.

However, many of you like to spend your Saturday evenings rolling around your lawn on your 327-horsepower John Deere Lawninator, enjoying the evening breeze while you mow, and maybe ruminating about the philosophical problems of the ages and even solving some of them while you work. And when you're done, you can look across the work of art that is your green, shiny lawn with the geometrically perfect lawnmower stripes, and say, "See what I hath wrought!" And that's cool too.

Now, raising a lawn has its challenges, just as everything else does. You'll see yards everywhere with rough spots, uneven, or with bare patches. Or, as happened to some unfortunate homeowners while we were having a drought, somebody threw a still-burning cigarette out a car window and started a fire that burned its way across several yards before it was extinguished. So remember: Maybe your lawn doesn't look the best right now, but things could always be worse.

A lot of folks who are juggling kids, work, household maintenance, and side jobs don't exactly have all the time in the world to sit down and study the fine points of lawn maintenance. I totally get that. This is why my lawn is a wreck. Also, chickens.

So I'm making this book short and sweet, and I hope reader-friendly, though occasionally I'll throw a little science your way. Because it's SCIENCE.

I'm going to lay out the best ways to make a great lawn without having to buy hundreds of dollars worth of chemicals and supplies. I'll talk about how to add fertility to the soil, how to water to keep the grass growing up and the water bill down, and how to keep your lawn mower serviced and working. And we'll pick up a lot of other helpful tips along the way.

Hey, if you like what you're reading, **please leave a review for this book. Every review is immensely helpful to an author, even if you just say, "Hey, cool book, five stars."** It lets others know that people think enough about the book to leave a review – and these books are often included in specials on different retailers that raise an author's profile. Believe me, we can always use a boost!

An agronomist from the University of Iowa looks over a selection of grass seed.

CHOOSING THE RIGHT GRASS FOR YOUR YARD

Turfgrasses, as the definition goes, are a type of grass that grows small and compact and benefits from being mowed. Turfgrasses are grown tightly together to create those broad swaths of green that become your gorgeous lawn. This tight-knit growth also helps your lawn resist the daily wear and tear of feet, dogs, and little kids – unless the little kids have shovels, and then you're falling into random pits in the yard.

But when you're building a yard, you really have to decide which kind of turfgrass will be best for your particular lawn.

First, you have to choose your grass by climate – cool season, warm season, or transition grasses.

Cool season grasses do well in the north. They're at their best in spring and fall, when temperatures are 60 to 70 degrees. In summer, cool-season grasses go dormant in the heat and drought, sometimes turning yellow or brown. In winter, they go dormant again, but they recover when spring warms them back up again, and then they're just as green as can be.

Warm season grasses do well in the south, enjoying the long, hot summers and short winters there. These grasses luxuriate in the heat, then go dormant and brown in winter. If they are hit with a bad cold snap, some of them even die off. Some warm-season grasses are overseeded in the fall with cool season grasses, just to add a little green and some winter reliability.

There's a belt across the middle of the country, most notably through West Virginia, Kentucky, Oklahoma, etc., called the transition area. Here, the winters are too cool for warm season grasses, and the summers are too hot for cool season grasses, leaving the poor lawnsman frustrated and befuddled. Grass mixes are often used in these areas, and may require a bit of extra effort to keep them lush. If you're in a transition area, you might check with your local University Extension service to see what grasses they recommend for your area. The University Extension service (and this goes not only for grasses, but for any aspect of horticulture and gardening) have all kinds of free pamphlets as well as a horticulturist on staff to answer all your questions. And their services are free, though a soil test will cost you a couple of bucks.

Cool-Season Grasses

Used mostly north of Zone 7, these grasses stay somewhat green in winter, usually in Zones 5 and 6, but can turn brown in summer when it's hot and dry. In 2011 we had a massive drought in the Midwest (even though we had a gigantic flood at the same time – welcome to Missouri), and everything turned brown and crackly in July, especially the grass (except in the floodplain, where it was pretty green). That was a strange year.

Cool-season grasses are fine textured and can be mowed at two or three inches high, and can be grown from seed or put down as sod. Northern grasses can be planted straight, as an all-bluegrass lawn, but they really work best if you buy them in combinations with other kinds of grasses. As I pointed out earlier, Nature hates a monoculture. If you buy several different types of grasses for your yard, you're in better shape. If you have a wet spring that brings a fungus that targets bluegrass, then your fescues and ryegrass keep on growing, so your lawn still stays green. Also, a grass mixture helps establish a new lawn. Some grass species are called "nurse" species because these grasses tend to grow up quickly, then offer shade and support to other grass species that germinate and grow more slowly. Ryegrass is an example of a nurse grass, and will grow up quickly and shades the slow-to-germinate bluegrass.

Here are a few kinds of cool-season grasses to pick from.

Kentucky Bluegrass (*Poa pratensis*)

Bluegrasses work best in areas where you want a lush, green turf, such as lawns, golf fairways, parks, or athletic fields. It loves full sun the best, and doesn't do well in shade. However, in the south, a little light shade will help this grass through the hot summer months.

Bluegrass tends to make up about 50 percent of most cool-season mixtures, and prefers to be cut at about 2 ½ inches, though newer varieties can be cut a little shorter. (Longer grass tends to be healthier, in this case, and also keeps weeds from growing.)

Bluegrass takes more work, water, and fertilizing, though newer varieties don't require as much work.

Bluegrass makes a dense, dark green lawn. It spreads by rhizomes – that is, though a rootlike stem that grows horizontally, sending out roots and stems – which helps the grass turn into a thick, lush mat. This is a hardy grass for cold areas.

Missouri fescue (*Fescue arundinacea*)

Also known as tall fescue. This particular species of grass is actually Kentucky 31, a variety that was developed after it was collected from a pasture in Kentucky in 1931. It's a good grass for poor, infertile soils. Missouri fescue is a bunch grass (that is, it grows in clumps, or bunches). If it's seeded thickly, makes a good, dense sod that bounces back nicely after drought.

One reason that fescue is such a tough grass is because about 90 percent of fescue has a microscopic fungus – an endophyte – growing inside the grass itself. (Technically, this fungus lives inside the *cells* of the plant.) This kind of grass is called an endophytic grass.

This partnership between the grass and fungus is symbiosis – a relationship between two different organisms that benefits both. Fescue is a very tough plant because of this endophyte. The fungus that lives inside the grass makes the grass bitter to grazing animals, diseases, and insects, so it keeps fescue healthy in conditions that would badly damage other grasses. In return, the fungus has a nice, safe place to live.

These kind of fescues are called endophytic fescues and sometimes sell at a higher price due to this resiliency.

Fine fescue (*Festuca rubra*)

Also called red fescue. These are often included in grass seed mixes – usually about 30 or 40 percent of the mix – because they're more shade and drought-tolerant than Kentucky bluegrass. They like shady areas and prefer low-traffic areas, and sprouts quickly. This fescue does not like wet soils, clay, extreme heat, or heavy wear.

Chewing Fescue (*Festuca rubra communtata*)

This is a kind of fine fescue that can take bad and acidic soils, and also tolerates shade, cold, and drought. This grass is best in shady lawns mixed with other grasses like Kentucky bluegrass. It's also great in low-maintenance areas, or areas that don't get much traffic, but it's wimpy in high-traffic areas and it takes a while to recover in damaged areas.

Chewing fescue is a little aggressive, so make sure it doesn't take over your stand of bluegrass. In acidic soils, keep an eye on it because it tends to develop thatch there.

Perennial Ryegrass (*Lolium perenne*)

This usually makes up a small portion of the grass seed mix, about 15 percent or so, because too much perennial ryegrass could keep other grasses from growing. Perennial ryegrass grows and matures quickly – you'll often see young shoots within three days of sowing – and so it's often used as a "nurse grass" to shade the grass seeds that are slower to germinate and grow (especially Kentucky bluegrass). Plus, it helps to hold the soil in place and keeps erosion down while the other grass is taking its sweet time to grow.

Perennial ryegrass is good in lawns, playing fields, or other high-traffic areas. It doesn't need a lot of maintenance. It's not as cold-tolerant as Kentucky bluegrass, and the tips of this grass often turn brown when it's mowed, as it's prone to "blade shredding." That is, cutting it will a dull blade on your lawn mower will leave ragged and torn edges on the grass blade.

Protip: Keep the blades on your mower sharp and clean so they will give your grass a nice, clean cut. Think of them the way you think of the razor you use to shave your face or legs – for painless results, keep them clean, and keep them sharp!

Bentgrass (*Agrostis palustris*)

This is a very fine-textured grass that's occasionally included in these cool-season mixtures, and by itself makes a velvety carpetlike turf. This is a very high-maintenance grass, seldom used for lawns. It grows very well in the Pacific Northwest, where it's cool and moist. A lot of golf courses use bentgrass because it can be mowed very short, down to a ¼ inch, and you'll see it a lot on putting greens, tennis courts, and bowling greens.

If you let bentgrass grow over an inch tall, the blades flop over and it grows sideways, like a boy who hasn't had his hair cut for a while. So you really have to stay on top of it unless you like that floppy look.

Bentgrass must be mowed frequently, watered frequently, and fertilized frequently. Oh yes, and it's prone to thatch, so be sure to aerate and dethatch it in early spring.

Annual Ryegrass (*Lolium multiforum*)

I'm including this more as a warning than a recommendation. If you are looking for a grass to grow in a permanent lawn, annual ryegrass is not it. This grass lives only for one season (that's why it's an annual, not a perennial), and its main uses are to build a temporary lawn, or to overseed a southern grass in order to keep some green in the winter lawn.

If you find a cheap seed mix that contains mostly annual ryegrass, then you're not getting your money's worth. The annual ryegrass will die out quickly, and next spring you're left with a sad-looking lawn full of holes. *Caveat emptor!*

preparation, proper fertilization and good seed are the most important steps toward a successful lawn. Read "10 Steps in Lawn Building," then select the mixture below, most suited to your needs. The results will please you.

Wyatt-Quarles CAROLINA
LAWN GRASS MIXTURE
F-60. W.-Q. CAROLINA MIXTURE of lawn grass seeds is an improvement on all the better mixtures offered heretofore at comparative

Warm Season Grasses

These tend to go dormant and brown during cold weather, and croak when the ground freezes, but during the long, hot southern summers they stay nice and green. Warm-season grasses have a course texture – that is, they have thick blades – but also can be mowed very short, down to an inch in height.

They're generally planted as sod, plugs, or sprigs, and are not planted in seed mixtures the way northern grasses are.

To help prevent winter-kill in warm-season grasses, apply a thin layer of sand to the grass in the fall. Check for drainage problems in your yard and fix them so the water won't puddle in your yard in winter. On your last mowing of the year, mow a little high so your grass has a bit of a buffer zone against the frosts and freezes of late fall.

Bermuda Grass (*Cynodon spp.*)
A very popular warm-season grass. Bermuda grass is low-

maintenance, coarse, puts up with poor soil and low mowing. Its roots go deep, making it heat and drought tolerant, and it's also salt tolerant. However, when the temperature drops below 55 degrees it will go brown and dormant. It doesn't tolerate shade. Bermuda grass can also be aggressive and take over areas outside your lawn, such as your garden. It spread through stolons, which are stems that grow above the ground, and rhizomes, which are stems that grow below the ground.

Bermuda grass works best in lawns (it is very good for high-traffic areas), athletic fields, parks, golf courses, and school playgrounds.

Bermuda grass is usually started with sprigs or plugs.

The new, improved varieties need more water and maintenance than the old ones; however, these grasses are less coarse, and they also stay greener in winter. They don't work in shade, though.

St. Augustine Grass (*Stenotaphrum scundatum*)

You can pull the stolons of St. Augustine grass out of lawns in an endless strand. If you keep pulling, eventually the yard unravels, and then you have to crochet it back together.

Kidding!

This is a more difficult grass to mow due to its very coarse texture, so you really have to keep the mower blades sharp with this one. However, it is shade-tolerant, so it can grow where your Bermuda grass won't.

St. Augustine grass makes a dense turf that won't let anything else grow up in your yard. It should be mowed to 2 to 4 inches tall. St. Augustine grass is not cold tolerant at all, and you'll need to mow, water, and fertilize it often during its peak growing season. It makes kind of a rough lawn, even with proper care.

Zoysia Grass (*Zoysia spp.*)

This stuff is crazy tough, is fine textured, and is easy to grow. It will build up thatch quite handily, so you'll have to aerate it or dethatch it in the early spring so it has time to recover during its peak growth.

You can grow it up north, but it will turn straw-colored in the winter. On the other hand, it doesn't totally die off in winter like many of these other warm-season grasses. It's very drought-resistant, though – almost a necessity, these days.

Zoysia is often called a "miracle grass" because it makes a dense turf, and can take heavy foot traffic. However, it takes a couple of seasons to fill in enough to look like a lawn, and it's a little prickly for bare feet. Once it's filled in, though, it's filled in for life. It doesn't need a lot of mowing, either – always a plus.

Zoysia is a great grass for the transition zone, where it's a little too hot for cool-season grasses and a little too cold for warm-season grasses. And, unlike other warm-season grasses, zoysia can be grown from seeds as well as sprigs and plugs.

Buffalo Grass (*Buchloe dactyloides*)

This is a grass I've really wanted to try for a long time. It's a native prairie species, extremely drought tolerant, heat tolerant, and, if grown to its full height of 8 to 10 inches, does not need to be mowed. It will look more like a turfgrass if you mow it at 3 to 4 inches.

You want to know how tough this grass is? Early fossil records reveal that buffalo grass has been around for at least *seven million years*. We're just tiny babies next to this stuff!

When I say drought tolerant, I mean it – buffalo grass can grow in areas that get only 10 to 15 inches of rainfall per year. Of course, it will go dormant under these conditions, and looks more cheery if you give it a little more water. But if you have very tough water restrictions, buffalo grass might be the way to go.

The seed is expensive – no doubt about that. Actually, this is partly because the seed burs are very big when compared to other grass seeds. It can also be started with sod or through plugs. Establishing buffalo grass can be tricky because this stuff is slow-growing and doesn't germinate as a dense stand as fescues do. And don't give this grass very much water at all – you'll kill it off!

But if you have an area that needs an intensively drought and heat tolerant grass in a place where you can't do a lot of mowing, this is the grass for you.

Bahiagrass (*Paspalum notatum*)

This is a coarse-textured, rugged grass that can be tough to get rid of once you're planted it. It spreads by seed and loves the hot, dry weather of Florida. It will grow in sandy, poor soil, spreads aggressively, is very durable, and is shade tolerant. In fact, it is very good in sandy soil because Bahiagrass has a huge root system that will pull every bit of water from the soil. Just mow this grass at two or three inches. The blades are tough, so you'll have to mow it often, and keep your mower blades sharp for best results.

Blue Grama Grass (*Bouteloua gracilis*)

This was a bit of a surprise to me because I always have known blue grama as a native prairie grass, not a turfgrass. The qualities that make it outstanding in the prairie – hardiness to both extremes of the thermometer, excellent drought tolerance, great erosion control, a perfect grass if you need a shortgrass meadow – all these qualities make it a natural for a low-maintenance natural turfgrass. If you have grazing animals, this grass has a lot of good nutrition for them. Blue grama is a great choice for sandy soils.

It takes a little management to grow it as a serviceable turf – but don't irrigate it or fertilize it much, because too much water or fertilizer will cause other grasses to intrude.

Blue grama is best if you use it to naturalize such things as the roughs of golf courses, or if you want a lawn that won't be mowed much. You can mow it to 1.5 to 3 inches tall. Irrigate this grass enough to prevent summer dormancy. Mix with buffalo grass for a good stand of native prairie grass.

Transition Areas

Transition areas cover a lot of areas where it tends to be too cool for warm-season grasses, but too hot for cold-season grasses. It's a heck of a deal. Perennial ryegrass is a good choice for this area, as well as tall fescue and zoysia. Tall fescue is a coarse grass (though newer varieties have a finer texture) but also very durable, making it great for heavily-traveled areas, play areas, dog runs, etc. It also takes some shade and stays green year round.

Really, you can use other grasses from both the cool season and the warm season sides. Look around and see what kinds of grasses the nice lawns in your area are using. Check with your local garden center to see what they're selling and what they recommend, and talk to your University Extension service for more recommendations that are best for your climate.

Woo your lady-love through lawn tennis! But preparing the lawn for said tournament is actually a lot of work.

CHOOSING THE BEST GRASS SEED

With grass seed, as with anything, you will have to pay a little money for the good stuff. Go to a reputable store, such as a lawn and garden store or a home improvement store, and shop early in the season for the best selection. Also, the germination rate with fresh seed will be a little higher than with old seed. The same goes for online retailers. Shop with highly-rated online sources. Garden Watchdog is a good source of knowledge about which online sources are worth working with.

Every bag of grass seed will have a label on it that tells you exactly what you're getting, and will include percentages. This label gives you a very helpful overview of what exactly you're getting in this bag of seed – and if it's worth your hard-earned cash to buy it.

Often, if a grass seed bag says "quick green" or "fast grass," then take a close look at the grass seed label. Dollars to donuts, you're going to have a lot of annual ryegrass in here. This seed will probably be very cheap. There's a reason for that: Annual ryegrass lasts for only one season, then gets killed off by the winter frost. Any spots that it greens up this year will be brown and bare next year. Sometimes the cheapest solution is not the best one.

So read on to find out how to translate that label on your bag o' grass seed, because if you buy a lot of grass seed, that label is going to be your new best friend.

HOW TO TRANSLATE YOUR GRASS SEED LABEL

The nice thing about the grass seed label is that they are required to list everything that's in the bag, and in what amounts. Hats off to the Federal Seed Act, as well as state seed laws, for keeping 'em honest.

Variety and Kind – This is the name of the seed, including the cultivar or release name, the species, and its common name.

Protip: Look for a specific cultivar name. That is, don't look for just "Kentucky Bluegrass" or "Fescue" but an additional name, like "Colt" or "Reubens" or "Waldina," and so forth. Named cultivars are often a great improvement over the original species.

Origin – In what state the seed was grown.

Germination Rate – What percentage of each seed variety will readily germinate under ideal conditions. Don't purchase seed with less than 70 percent germination. The higher the germination, the better.

Pure Seed – The percent, by weight, of each grass variety and kind.

Other Crop Seed – Other commercially grown grass crop. Sometimes you get a little orchard grass or timothy grass mixed up in your grass seed. However, this percentage should be zero, or one percent at the most.

Inert Matter – How much of the material in this bag that is plant debris, chaff, dirt, or other materials that are not seed. This should be less than four percent. HOWEVER, some grass seed includes fertilizer or mulch with the seed. In these cases, the inert matter percentage will be much higher.

Weed Seed -- The percentage of weed seed – that is, any seed that's not pure or crop seed. In an ideal world, this would be zero, but there's always a few weed seeds that sneak through the screening process, so look for a value of less than one percent.

Noxious Weeds -- These are weeds that are hard to control. If the grass seed contains noxious weeds, they have to be listed by name. These are restricted by state.

Guaranteed Analysis – If a bag of seed includes fertilizer, it's required to have a guaranteed analysis of the fertilizer and any ingredients meant to amend the soil. All fertilizer labels use an N-P-K ratio – that is, the proportion of nitrogen (N), Phosphorus (P), and Potassium (K). These reflect each nutrient's percentage by weight.

Test Date – This was when the seed was tested. Try to purchase grass seed that was tested within the last 12 months.

Sell By Date – Sell by date is listed by state. Check your state's date for the freshest seed!

PREPARING THE SITE

An old-fashioned soil testing kit. These days it's just easier to send your little boxes of soil to the University Extension.

SOIL SAMPLES FOR YARDS

Taking soil samples is a topic often overlooked, since it doesn't exactly lend itself to colorful graphics or splashy headlines ("Dirt! Test its cation exchange capacity today!"). Still, a soil test every three or four years is a necessary part of lawn care. One doesn't just look at the soil and say, "Whoa, gotta fix that low potassium level." Instead, one might notice a lawn that's not doing so hot, even though you've been fertilizing it.

That's why taking a soil sample is so important. Soil changes when fertilizer, mulch, sulfur or lime is added, or when minerals leach out of it. But, more important, you can find out exactly what nutrients are in your soil – and what your soil lacks – and then you can find out what soil amendments to add to fix the lack. Or, you can change your fertilizing regimen to boost those minerals that your soil lacks, while cutting back on the minerals your soil already has in abundance. At any rate, taking a soil test allows you to adjust the fertilizing regiment for your grass, which, in the long run, saves you money and greatly improves your soil (and the looks of your lawn).

Fall is a good time to take a soil sample – and you avoid the spring rush. So, to take a sample, the first thing to do is to get a little box from your local university extension center (or several boxes, if you are sampling several different areas – that is, if you were taking soil samples for your lawn and garden both, then you'd get two boxes, one for each. Gardens will need a fertilizing regimen that's different from lawns.). Carefully read the instructions that the University Extension gives you. Fill in the appropriate information on the side of that little box. Do this before you dig, since it's harder to write on the box once the soil's inside it.

Side note: I've always preferred to use my local university extension service for soil tests (and pretty much everything else). They're local, they're within budget, but they also understand the soil in your state and within your county.

Collecting samples.

Get a clean trowel or auger and a clean bucket to collect the soil in. Go to the garden or lawn where you plan to collect the sample. Check the soil for moisture by picking up a handful of soil, gently squeezing it into a ball, then release it. If the soil crumbles easily in your hand, then it's dry enough to sample. If the soil stays in the ball – or, worse, if it drips – wait until the soil dries to take your sample.

You'll be taking samples from 10 to 15 random spots around your yard. If you happen to have a soil probe, this part is easier. If you don't, then you'll need a shovel or a spade.

Set the shovel or spade into the soil -- over 7 inches deep -- and throw out that first shovelful. Then, at the back of the hole (where the shovel's back rested), set the shovel in again, cutting a slice that measures from a half-inch to an inch thick and 7 inches deep. Pull off the thin root-layer of grass at the top and place the soil in the pail. Then repeat that step five or six times within the area of your garden, lawn or farmland. Take one soil sample for every thousand feet of land. (If you have a huge lawn, you may need two boxes.)

If you live near a gravel road, don't take samples near it. The gravel on the road is limestone, and its dust will make your soil test come up highly alkaline, even if the soil is actually acidic.

Finally, take different samples from areas with different purposes. That is, take one sample for the garden, one for the lawn, and one for the orchard, since each has a different fertilization regimen.

When you have taken samples from all of the random spots, mix all the samples together in the bucket until you have crumbs of dirt – no big clods. Then scoop out enough soil to fill the box, close it, and take it to the local soil testing site. You'll pay a small fee for processing.

Results generally come back in two or three weeks, with a description of your soil's needs that you can start using when next year's planting season begins. You should get a listing of what nutrients are in the soil -- and which ones aren't. The soil test report also will show you the amount of organic matter in the soil, which also is a great part of the soil's structure.

You'll soon get a report on your soil's condition, with suggestions at the bottom to help you out. You can also talk to your University Extension agent for even more suggestions and ideas. Then you're on your way to correcting any imbalances in your soil, which your lawn will definitely thank you for.

The "Velvet=Lawn"

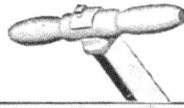

Hitch up ol' January and let's fix up some soil!

IMPROVING THE SOIL

So your house is finished at last, and the lumber and scraps and nails have been cleared away, and now you have a yard with patches of all these different soils in varying colors. Or, you're completely renovating your lawn and have killed all your grass and weeds completely dead. So now what do you do with this poor, barren yard? Well, that's a good question.

If you've had extensive construction work done on this house, then you're going to have to do a little work on the soil that remains. Sometimes you have the bad luck to have what I call "subdivision soil." This kind of soil – the ground-up, compacted subsoil that's sometimes left after construction – often has very little of the original topsoil on it.

Here in Missouri, some of our subsoil is yellow and gray clay that cakes and clumps up very badly. It's a kind of plastic clay – the kind that sticks to your shoes after a rain, the kind that you can even make a little sculpture out of, if you are so inclined. When you dig in subdivision soil, your shovel often strikes rocks, which is jarring. Drainage is very bad in this kind of soil due to all the compaction from heavy vehicles, and of course because it's clay. Water will puddle in this soil, and young trees often do very poorly here. White pines in subdivision soil will develop big gaps in their foliage and grow up to be all spindly.

Talk to your landscape contractor about the soil, first off. They'll know the most about it, since they've already been digging in it. If the soil is very bad – or if you simply want to get off to a good start – have some good top soil trucked in and put it all over your yard.

This is the time when you go back to my chapter about doing a soil test, read that, and get your soil tested. Talk to your University Extension horticulturist or agrarian or soil boss about how to fix up your soil. They might even come out and take a look at your soil on-site if you ask nicely. Ask them about organic ways to improve the soil. They should give you a hand.

There are a number of soil issues that I don't cover in this book – desert soils, sandy soils, fragipan, alkaline soils – because the only kind of soil I've dealt with in my lifetime is Missouri clay and loam. That's why I highly recommend supplementing my advice in this book with their local expertise.

If you really want to get a good start with your yard, add organic material to your topsoil -- compost, processed manure (not straight-from-the-barnyard manure, as it will smell bad and have weed seeds), bone meal, and an old-fashioned soil additive called greensand. Try to get about three or four inches of amendments on your yard, and dig them in as much as possible. Rent a good-quality tiller if you're doing this work yourself, one that will really mix the soil for you and pulverize the big bumps and clumps.

Once that's all tilled in, you might have to go over the ground with the rake several times until the surface is smooth and beautifully flat, and all the holes are filled with soil and tamped solid, and all the big clods and lumps are gone.

When we worked on the baseball fields with Parks and Rec, we did several things to get the ground in tip-top condition for grass seed or sod. First, everybody would go out with five-gallon buckets to pick up all the little rocks and clods lying on the soil's surface. Then they'd rake the ground. Then we'd pick up more little rocks.

This level of detail is not always necessary for your average yard, especially if you're a lassiez-faire kind of lawn person. Like me. However, if you want turf that's very good, pick up all of the little rocks and clods. A very finely-pulverized soil will help your grass seeds touch the soil granules and grow nicely. Removing the rocks will help in this endeavor.

If you have pits in your yard, add in soil from higher points in the yard, or have good topsoil brought in to fill it. Tamp in the soil firmly – otherwise, as the soil settles, you'll get a depression there. In some cases, it might be a good idea to actually dig into this depression and see how far down it goes. Sometimes you might find a small cavern underground, or an old cistern that needs to be filled and tamped (or shown to the local archeological society). Correct the source of the soil slump so it doesn't keep slumping.

Also, take time to bring the soil up to a slope all around the house's foundation, if the building contractors haven't done this already, and have somebody grade the land. The soil should slope away from your foundation at least at a 1:50 slope – that is, the grade of the land should slope down one foot when you're 50 feet away from your house.

Make sure there are no places in your yard where the water will puddle. As you know, long-term low areas next to the house can affect the foundation. Also, bringing the soil up against the house will help keep it from pulling away from the side of the house, which can create trouble with the foundation. Putting soil right against the house also keeps water out and helps to keep crickets and fall insects from coming into your house and taking up residence by the hundreds in the laundry room or your dining room window.

PLANTING A GORGEOUS LAWN

Of course, your climate and your soil will affect your grass choices, as well as planting times.

Cool-season grasses should be planted in late summer or early fall. This time of year, the soil is nice and warm, which aids in germination, and any annual weeds that come up with the grass are killed off by frost. Not only that, but the grass has three seasons to get established -- fall, winter, and spring – before summer's heat and drought strike. Then you don't have to constantly water the grass as you would have if the grass had been planted in spring.

(P.S. Winter does count as a growing season. In all but the very coldest days of winter, roots are quietly growing underground, even when the soil is frozen.)

Be sure to sow your fall seeds at least four weeks before the first frost date. Six weeks before the first frost is best, so they can get their root system growing.

Warm-season grasses, on the other hand, are best planted in spring so they can luxuriate in the delicious summer heat before that awful cold sets in.

Now, sometimes you have no choice but to plant at some other time of year. I've heard that you can plant seed even in winter, throwing it on the snow cover, which would be great for even coverage – the snow would show up any gaps in your sowing. Of course, you should throw out seed while it's snowing so the falling snow can cover your grass seeds and hide them from the birds! The seeds melt down with the snow, not germinating, and they get cuddled in with the ground very well for early spring, then they grow when they're ready. And you can still plant grass in spring or even in summer (if you're able to keep up with keeping it watered) if you need to.

Really, if you can work with the plants – that is, keep them watered, or throw a little straw over them to protect them from the harsh summer sun – then you should be fine. Plants are really forgiving, when it comes to it. And if some of the grass seedlings die off for some reason, it's still okay. Just re-seed the bare patches later.

When you're dealing with living things, whether it be with plants, animals, or even humans (*cough*kids!*cough*), sometimes they turn out to be contrary, stubborn, bull-headed, or goofballs, and they don't act the way you want them to. That's the way it goes. Just try again later.

Seeding the lawn
Generally, grass seed should be sown at about 3 pounds per

1,000 square feet – but each mix and variety will differ, so check the package for the recommended amount.

April and May are the best months for seeding the lawn, but you can do it most any month where you get a decent amount of rainfall, or any time you're able to keep the lawn watered. I've seen good effects from seeding in the bleak midwinter, on top of snow. Obviously you can't take the seeder out when there's snow on the ground, but if you hand-sow, you can see where the seed falls and then add in more. (If you go this route, seed before a big snowstorm comes in so it gets covered up so the birds don't eat it.)

Personally, if I had a big construction area that needed to be seeded, I would seed everything in white clover and let it fix nitrogen into the soil. Then, the next spring, I'd kill it off with some broadleaf herbicide and put down grass seed. Annnnnnnd this is why I will never live anywhere there's a Homeowner's Association, because they'd probably run me out of town on a rail.

Maybe I should call this book the Redneck's Guide to Lawns. Well, actually no, because I know a lot of rednecks and we just don't do lawns ... because we need someplace to drive the four-wheeler. Next!

(I really shouldn't joke about rednecks because they're all armed.)

But seriously, if you're in a place where you *don't* have neighbors or HOAs that tell you what you need to put in your lawn, plant white clover to put nitrogen into the soil. Leave it in until it's time to reseed, then kill it off with broadleaf herbicide, or, for organic folks, use industrial-strength vinegar.

(If you use industrial-strength vinegar, be sure to wear gloves and goggles. This is much, much more acidic than the vinegar you put on your salad, and I guarantee it will burn you. It's a good herbicide, though. So use with caution.)

After you kill off the clover, mow off the dead clover at the lawnmower's lowest setting, then leave the rest there as a mulch. Then reseed the yard with grass seed, raking in the seed when you're done.

You might have to use broadleaf herbicide on any remaining patches of clover a couple of times to kill it off, or spot-spray rogue patches. At any rate, the nitrogen that the clover will add to your yard is valuable. The clover roots help hold the soil in place, and keep nitrogen in the yard for a little while longer, and add humus to the soil as they decay. (Humus is organic material, and necessary to keep soil abuzz with life, which in turn helps invigorate your grass roots in a million ways.)

Also, that nitrogen is the element that you want in your yard for your grass. Nitrogen is what makes grass lush and green. And to have that nitrogen actually below the soil's surface, naturally, instead of through some chemical fertilizer on top of the soil, is very effective, because it's right at root level where the grass roots need it most.

How to sow grass seed

A small, pushable sower is the best way to go. You can use it for grass seed as well as granular fertilizer. It's easy to use and doesn't make a racket, so you can think deep philosophical thoughts while you're walking up and down the yard, if you're so inclined.

The trick with sowing is to spread the grass seed evenly with little overlap.

First, find out how far out your spreader will throw the grass seed. Fill your spreader with grass seed, take it out in the yard and walk a little way at the pace you plan to use while putting down seed. Then get out the tape measure and measure how wide the area of coverage is, where the grass seed falls. There will be an area where the grass seed is not thick, and this will be where you will overlap.

Then write down that that measurement of maximum coverage – let's say your area of maximum coverage is five feet. Get some of those little marker flags at the local DIY store. Go to the far edge of your yard and set them five feet apart all the way across. Then go to the other end of your yard and place those flags five feet apart, so they line up with the ones on the other side. These will be your guides when you're sowing your seed. It's very hard to keep a straight path when you're sowing, and these flags will be invaluable in keeping your lines straight and your seed from overlapping too much.

Then, when you're done going east to west, pick up the flags and repeat the process going north to south. This will give you even coverage all over your yard.

Rake the grass in to a depth of a quarter-inch. Or, spread a thin layer of compost over the grass all over the yard for added organic material and nutrition for the grass. Then, if you have a roller, roll the lawn to get excellent grass-to-soil contact. If you don't have a roller, throw down straw to shade the grass and hide it from birds.

Hand-sowing grass seed

Sometimes you just need to throw out some seed over a small area. Instead of dragging out the spreader, hand-sow it.

Hand-sowing evenly can be a little tricky. Choose a day with as little wind as possible, as any wind will sow your grass where it wants it to go – into flowerbeds, into your hair, etc. Again, you'll sow north to south, then east to west for best coverage.

Fill your hand with grass seed and hold it close to the ground. Make a circular motion from right to left and then back again, letting the seeds fall from your fingers as evenly as possible. You'll have to experiment for best results.

Or a little hand-spreader will also work in these situations.

It's the size of a little box, and has a crank on the side to scatter the seed far and wide.

After sowing the grass seed

There are several schools of thought on this. Some people roll the lawn after the grass seed is sown. Rolling will press the seed into the soil and give it a good connection with the ground for good germination. Others, preferring to avoid compacting the soil, will simply water it in and throw straw over the top to shade the seed and keep birds from eating it.

Water the grass evenly, keeping the ground moist but not soggy. Two or three times a day seems to work best. Stop watering when you see puddles starting to form on the soil.

Three or four days after you plant your seed, you'll see a fine mist of green over the ground's surface, and you can cut back on watering. About two weeks after that you'll see what kind of lawn you're going to have. Add grass seed to any bare or thin patches. Water the soil liberally every day if the weather is dry.

Don't mow until the new grass is at least three inches high – even then, raise the mower deck high and be sure to clip off just the top of the grass. Don't clip it close until the grass begins to thicken up. But even then, never shear the grass. You should always have about two inches of grass growing for best results (unless you have those warm-season grasses that prefer a short haircut, like bentgrass).

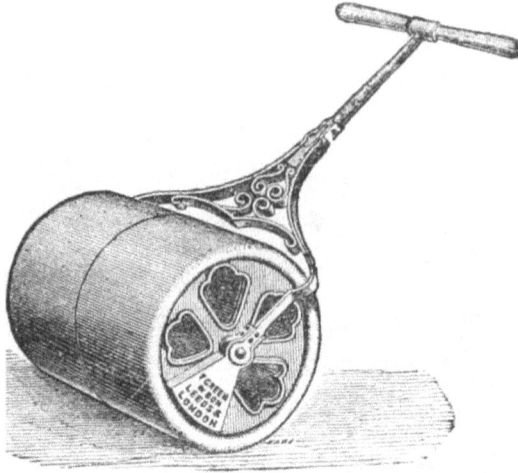

Roll out the barrel!

THE LOWDOWN ON SOD

Sod is instant gratification for your lawn. (Well, maybe it's not completely instant gratification, as you still need to do prep work to make the lawn ready to receive it.) Of course, being instant gratification, sod costs more to purchase and install.

On the other hand, after a day or two of work, plus a week of just-right watering, you get a luscious, thick green turf that looks like magic.

The very nice thing about sod is that somebody else – specifically, a team of people who knows a LOT about growing grass – has prepared this grass for the last 14 to 18 months, seeding it, feeding it, and blasting every weed that even tries to show its spindly head. So basically you're paying to have a professional's lawn installed at your house. Kind of a sweet deal!

Sod is also convenient. You can install it pretty much any time during the growing season. You don't have to worry about weeds popping up the way you would when you're sowing grass seed.

In the south, sod is often your main choice – some warm-season grasses (Bermuda grass, zoysia, or centipede grass) can't be grown from seed, but only via sprigs, plugs, or sod.

Now, if your lawn is shady, check to make sure you're getting shade-tolerant sod. These lush sod fields are grown in full sun with not a tree in sight, and the grass strains they use for these fields are for full sun. However, some sod is grown exclusively for shade, so be sure to tell your sod salesman about the shade conditions in your yard so you can get the best turf for your buck. Shade-tolerant sod is great around trees.

Sod can cover a multitude of faults. It chokes out weeds. Sod is great if you have a slope that you need to cover quickly before it erodes away. And it's ready to go in half the time compared to seeded lawns.

Or, if you have a bare spot in your yard where grass doesn't want to grow, cut it out and sod it. It costs more but it's an advantage. My father-in-law did that down at the lake. He got two rolls of sod, cut out the grass, laid the sod out, watered it, pff, done.

Buying Sod

You can buy sod at a nursery, a garden center, or directly from the sod farm itself. Be sure to do your homework when you're buying sod, however, so you can make sure you're getting a quality product.

Shop around for sod because it varies in price. It often depends on the farm it comes from. Sometimes if you call around, you might find there's two dollars difference per roll. Prices are all over the place. But check on quality before buying. Here are some pointers.

1) Measure your yard. You won't buy a new carpet without having measured your living room, so measure the space where you want to lay sod and calculate the square footage. Some lawns are irregular – that's fine, don't kill yourself with math. Get a close approximation of the total square footage, then add about 5 or 10 percent onto that so the sod installers will have enough leeway to cut and shape the sod to fit your irregular lawn.

2) Buy local sod. If you buy from a sod farmer in the area, you know that you'll be buying grass that does well in your climate and soil. This grass will do better than something that's shipped from out of state.

3) Order sod a week before you plan to lay it. This gives the grower time to cut and ship a good product. Also, don't order more than a week ahead. The sod should not sit out for more than 48 hours after it's delivered, or you'll start getting brown edges. Fresh sod is best.

4) Check the sod. Unroll a few sections of sod in your delivery and check for weeds, insects, diseases. A good company will deliver a clean product. If you see any of these things in your sod, send it back. You want clean grass; you aren't paying for sod so you can

fight dollar spot or grubs for the rest of your life. Also, check for signs of drying out – where the edges are browning or curling. It's not your job to bring sod back to life. Finally, check the roots to make sure they're white and moist. The sod should be cool to the touch. Sod that's been sitting around for a while will start to compost itself, killing the grass. These rolls, when you unroll them, gives you grass that's been darkened by the composting process. So if you can feel heat coming off the rolls, move on!

5) Also, the grass and its roots and soil should be thick enough to unroll and pick up without breaking. One time when I was at Parks, I was helping to lay sod at one of the baseball fields. The shipment we got was cut surprisingly thin. Some pieces would just come apart as we unrolled them, and we had to do our best to batten them together. I don't think we were able to send that shipment back, because we were on a tight deadline to finish that field (and the sod was probably from one of the boss's friends – so it goes).

Installing and Watering Sod

Once again, don't lay sod before you've prepared the soil. Add topsoil and till it in if the soil is really bad, do a soil test, add and till in those good organic soil amendments that your soil test results recommends, level and grade your soil (have at least a 1:50 slope away from your foundation), pick up any rocks on the ground. Then you're good to go.

It's best if you start working as soon as the sod shows up. If for some reason you have to wait, have the delivery people put the sod in the shade, and mist the rolls so they don't dry out. You can keep it rolled up for 24 or even 48 hours after delivery, but don't press your luck.

Tools:

A sharp utility knife, for cutting the sod to fit

A wheelbarrow for trucking it around

A water-filled roller, to roll the sod so it makes good contact with the ground

Stakes for VAMPIRES. No, the stakes are to secure sod that

you put on slopes

A piece of plywood to stand on while you're installing your sod (this eases compaction on the sod you've just laid)

Flags. If you've had a sprinkler system installed in your yard, walk through now and flag every sprinkler head in the yard. You'll need to cut the sod so the sprinkler heads will be able to pop up when they're turned on.

Now you're ready to start!

Find a nice, straight edge to start from, such as a sidewalk or a driveway. If you don't have a straight edge, make one by stretching a string on stakes in a straight line across the middle of your yard, and start laying sod on both sides of it.

Gently moisten the soil as you work so the grass roots in the sod make contact with moist ground. Then unroll the sod and batten it up against the straight line you're starting with. Set down the next roll so the end is directly touching the end of the previous roll, then unroll it. Then push the roll so its end is touching, but not overlapping, the other end. You want to make a nice smooth carpet with no gaps. Overlaps will make huge bumps in the yard that will bounce your lawnmower around. Gaps will leave brown areas where the crabgrass can pop through.

The sod can take a little rough handling, but don't go overboard and tear it. It's tough to batten together a torn piece.

Once you have the first row of sod laid, start the second row by laying it in a brick pattern. This keeps you from having long lines going across your lawn. Cut the sod around the edges of the lawn so it fits, and use these extra pieces to fill in areas where the sod doesn't quite meet up, or where you have to cut out an area that looks bad for one reason or another. Like a quilter, if you find a gap, set in a piece of sod that's cut to fit the hole. Keep aside a few rolls of sod in a shady place, and use these rolls for repairs.

If you're working on a slope, lay the sod across the slope, not up and down it. This helps to keep erosion down. Also, if the slope is particularly tricky, use stakes to hold the sod in place until it roots. Of course, mark each stake with a bit of red paint (landscaper's spray paint is handy for this) so you can get every single stake out BEFORE you mow.

Use the plywood, or a wide board, to kneel on if you have to work on the newly-laid sod. This helps distribute your weight evenly across the sod.

This is hot, dusty work. It's not so bad in the morning, but once the sun starts climbing, you start to feel the heat. Be sure to have your water or your sports drink nearby.

If you start to feel dizzy or lightheaded, get into some shade and take a few minutes to cool off. Heatstroke and heat exhaustion are serious matters – if you do any kind of long-term work in the summer heat, be aware of the warning signs. One year during an especially hot August that was filled with 95- and 100-degree days, one man died of heat exhaustion while mowing his yard. Don't become a statistic.

Once you've laid the sod, fill your roller halfway with water, then roll over the sod at a 90 degree angle to the direction you laid the sod. If you've laid a very large area, roll a section, water that section in, then move to the next section and repeat. While you're rolling, walk carefully so you don't accidentally pull up corners of the sod – or, worse, pull up a corner and then roll over it with the roller before you know what you've done.

And then, water. If you have a sprinkler system installed under the sod, now you can use it. If not, you'll have to use a lot of sprinklers, or some really dedicated people with hoses. Water deeply, giving your new sod 3 to 4 inches of water in its initial watering. Be especially sure to water out to the very edges of your new lawn, paying close attention to the edges of the sod. To check to be sure the water has penetrated, lift a corner of sod here and there and make sure the soil underneath is wet, then gently firm it back down.

Water the sod every day for the first week. Pay attention to the corners and edges – those are always first to dry out.

The roots start growing into the soil after the first week, so you won't have to water so much – maybe every other day. Watch the color of the sod carefully when you dial back the water. If it stays green, great. If it doesn't look as green, keep up the daily waterings for a little while longer. After three weeks, if all is well, you should be able water just a couple of times a week and be fine. (Of course, if you get a lot of rain, or if you're hit with an incredible drought, adjust the watering schedule accordingly.)

MAINTAINING YOUR LAWN

MOWING LAWN NEAR SEVENTY-NINTH STREET.

FIVE ORGANIC WAYS TO A BEAUTIFUL LAWN

Personally, I prefer having an organic lawn, but that's mainly because I have kids, chickens, a dog, and a cat, as well as various rabbits, squirrels, an occasional possum, voles, shrews, garter snakes, all kinds of birds, and of course those bugs I like so much. When I go outside, the chickens some running up, and usually the dog will come trotting out, and the cat comes over, and sometimes there's a rabbit off at the edge of the lawn eating some fallen apples, or a danged squirrel stealing my apples in the tree.

At any rate, I find it very pleasant to be surrounded by all these animals (except for the apple-stealing squirrel), and they all hang out together (except for the cat, who starts stalking the rabbit so I have to put him inside) and it's a very pleasant thing for me to sit on the stoop and talk to them.

That's why I don't use chemicals on the yard. That, and I'm lazy, preferring to sit and talk to chickens instead of going to the local farm store to buy a bag of weed and feed.

FIRST, stop bagging your grass clippings, and let them fall to the ground when you mow. By doing this, you can use 20 to 25 percent less fertilizer on your yard. Clippings contain 4 percent nitrogen, 1 percent phosphorus and 3 percent potassium, as well as trace minerals.

Clippings also act as a light mulch between mowings. They keep grass from drying out, shade out weed seeds, and keep thatch from accumulating. Since grass clippings are 75 to 80 percent water, they wither and get out of sight quickly.

Use your leaves in the same way – shred them and rake them into the grass. Mulching mowers are the best for this. Otherwise, you may have to make several passes over the leaves to chop them up well.

Grass clippings do not cause thatch, but if thatch – a mat of grass roots and creeping runners – already exists in your yard, clippings can make the thatch problem worse. Rent or borrow a dethatcher to fix the problem.

Use a mulching mower. This kind of mower will cut the clippings into smaller bits than a regular mower would. Fewer clipping, less raking, less work. Mulching mowers do their best job when you mow no more than 1 inch to 1.5 inches off. More than that and they tend to clog up.

Don't let the clippings clump – rake them up and put them on your garden. It makes a nice, soft mulch that unfortunately vanishes after a month or two. So keep adding it. (I pick up extra clippings at the landfill. Just be sure the grasses you're picking up haven't been sprayed with herbicides. I get those with small weeds and clovers among the grass – no herbicides there.)

SECOND, sow endophytic grasses. Endophytic grasses contain a fungus that lives inside fescue and ryegrass in a symbiotic relationship. The fungus has a nice home, and the grass tastes nasty to diseases, bugs, and animals – the same way that fungus makes moldy bread taste awful. These endophytic grasses are great lawn grasses, since they are resistant to the diseases that regular grasses get. No bugs, no fungus. These are more expensive than regular grasses, of course, and you'll need to plant them as soon as possible to be sure the fungus remains viable inside the grass seeds.

THIRD, mow the grass high, at least 2 ½ or 3 inches tall, so it shades and mulches itself. Tall grass shades out weeds and keeps the roots cool. When you cut the grass low, then it gets stressed and is more likely to catch diseases.

Also, tall grass is more pleasant to walk and lie down in.

FOURTH, maintain your lawn mower. Keep the blade sharp and balanced so grass is cut cleanly, instead of torn. Change the crankcase oil when needed, clean the carburetor filter, and check the spark plug. Mowing will go a lot faster and more efficiently. Also, guess what, you'll save gas.

FIFTH, skip the chemical additives you give it. Instead, mulch the grass by spreading compost, well-rotted manure, Bradfield fertilizer (with the alfalfa in it) or greensand on it. Get the spreader, pile in the goods, then walk up and down and spread the good stuff all over your yard. Feed the soil. This way you give the soil long-lasting additives that will slowly release the nutrients your grass, and the beneficial soil organisms, need. In return, the grass will show you how happy it is.

Then get some local earthworms at the bait shop (or better yet, their eggs) and dig them into the soil all over the lawn. Water all of it in. Let the worms aerate the soil and turn everything under for you. Healthy soil has lots of earthworms, but the ground won't be healthy unless you feed it the organic materials that it needs. Chemicals will kill the earthworms, making your soil hard as a brick, which means you have to rent an aerator more often. Why do all that work when nature will do it for you?

So there's five organic ways to keep the yard in good shape – and you can let your children and pets play on it without worry.

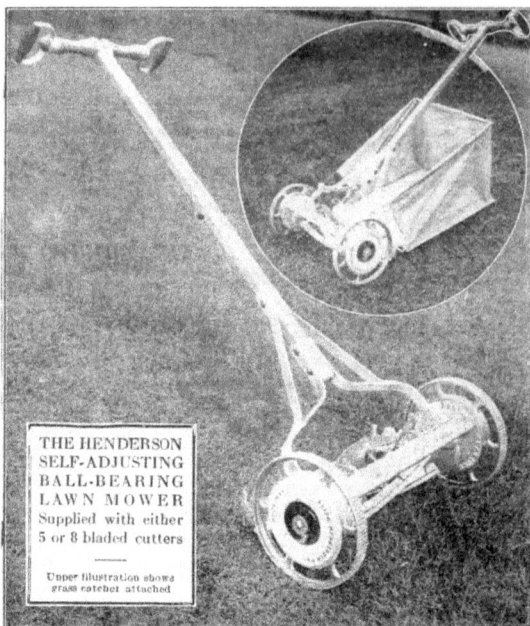

THE HENDERSON
SELF-ADJUSTING
BALL-BEARING
LAWN MOWER
Supplied with either
5 or 8 bladed cutters

Upper illustration shows
grass catcher attached

DON'T BAG IT –
LET GRASS CLIPPINGS FALL
WHERE THEY MAY

Walt Whitman, the Civil War poet, would have a hard time with today's world. He wrote:

> **A child said, *What is the grass?* fetching it to me with full hands;**
> **How could I answer the child? I do not know what it is any more than he.**

The harried homeowner, burdened with a power rake, 50 pounds of chemicals and a 75-foot garden hose coiled around his shoulder, shouts, "It's a dad-blamed nuisance, that's what it is!"

Though Whitman is inviting your soul to observe, at its ease, a spear of summer grass, you have to turn him down. You have to go out there and spray and water and mow and fuss with the grass.

Our university extension center, as well as university extensions around the nation, have several suggestions on how to make your lawn care chores a little easier, while saving money on fertilizers, keeping thatch down and allowing good grass to grow with less labor.

University Extension centers around the country have a program called "Don't Bag It." They are encouraging homeowners to stop bagging their grass clippings. Instead, they should let their grass clippings fall back into the grass.

The benefits of recycling your grass clippings are many. When you let the clips fall where they may, you can use 20 to 25 percent less fertilizer on your yard. This is because clippings contain 4 percent nitrogen, 1 percent phosphorus and 3 percent potassium, as well as trace minerals.

Clippings also act as a light mulch between mowings, which keeps grass from drying out, shades out weed seeds, saves on landfill space, and keeps thatch from accumulating.

"Now wait a minute," says the indignant homeowner, because that 75-foot hose over his shoulder is getting mighty heavy. "You can't do that. That's how you get all that thatch."

Well, it depends. Thatch is actually a mat of grass roots and creeping runners -- not clippings. Grass clippings are 75 to 80 percent water. Once the clipped grass withers, which doesn't take long, the remaining bit of grass decomposes quickly. To see for yourself, leave some clippings on your garden border, and watch them for a week or two.

Now, if thatch is already present in the yard, then yes, grass clippings will add to the problem. Rent or borrow a dethatcher, fix that problem, and then you'll be able to let the clippings fall where they may.

Don't let the clippings clump, such as when you mow after a rain, or when the grass grows too high, since this will shade out the grass underneath. If you must mow after rain, let the clippings dry a little before you rake them out. If the grass gets too high, as it does when you're on vacation, handle it this way: raise the mower blade to its highest setting and cut the grass once. Let the clippings dry. Then, lower the blade to your preferred setting and cut again, this time in a different direction. This will chop and scatter the clippings sufficiently.

Finally, invest in a mulching mower. These mowers are great for cutting grass or chopping up all those extra leaves in fall. (An old mulching mower can turn fifteen bags of leaves into one inch of mulch over a 15x25 garden. It sure beats bagging them.)

Don't you love natural solutions?

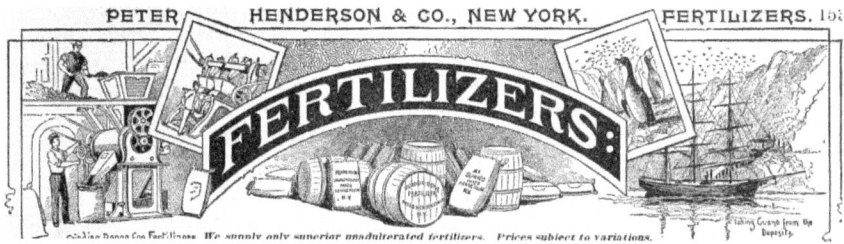

FEEDING THE LAWN

Take it easy when you're fertilizing your grass in summer. Some fertilizer is needed at this time. However, overapplication (especially of nitrogen) is definitely a problem, causing overly green and juicy grass that insects can really sink their mandibles into. Overly fertilized grass also causes too much growth, resulting in lawn-cutting nightmares.

The best time to fertilize cool-season grasses is in August and September, and in late fall, from October through December. This fertilization practice creates a hardier and tougher grass with a deeper root system and slower growth.

Weed and Feed

Back in my pre-chicken days, when I first moved into my house which had a nice lawn, I decided to use some weed and feed. Weed and Feed is simply a broadleaf weed killer mixed with fertilizer, in granular form. (And if you're a real beginner, as I was at the time, a broadleaf weed killer simply kills weeds that are not grasses. Grasses have narrow leaves, while broadleaves plants – clover, dandelion, plantain, ground ivy, etc. – have broad leaves.)

Reading the package, I was a little surprised at all the preparation that was necessary before I put the weed and feed down. Three days before, mow the lawn. Two days before, water the lawn. Then be sure to apply the weed and feed while the dew is on the grass – that allows the chemical to adhere better to the weeds it's meant to kill. And for heaven's sake, apply this chemical no more than twice a year!

I discovered the lure of "just a little more" while pushing the spreader around the yard. "Aw, come on," the little devil on my shoulder said. "If you put a little extra on the grass, it will be really weed-free. And this will be the first time that you've have had a green yard!" (My former yard at my previous house was purple in spring due to all the henbit, then white from the clover, then the rest of the year it was brown.)

Then the little angel whacked the devil with a 2x4. "Always read and follow label directions!" she shouted, "Mrs. *Gardening Columnist!*" So I made one pass over the whole lawn and that was it, I swear.

Later I found that you can make a second application if the weeds are excessive, but adding too much weed and feed will damage your grass. So now you know.

If you have newly-seeded grass, don't use broadleaf weed killers until the new grass has been mowed three times. Wait one month after you apply the weed killer to seed new grass. Broadleaf herbicide does go after non-grasses, but too much can burn regular grass.

You know, the lawn did look better after I'd applied the weed and feed. After that little adventure, I started moseying down the fertilizer aisle a lot, eyeing what else was available. It was kind of strange not to be singing, "I Fought the Lawn and the Lawn Won" every time I stepped out into the yard. But it was kind of nice, too.

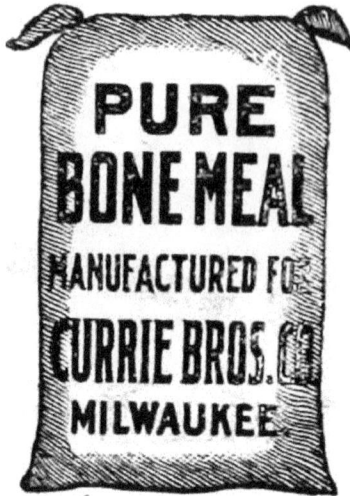

WHAT TO LOOK FOR IN LAWN FERTILIZERS

"He who fertilizes best fertilizes least."

I don't know if that's true or not, as it's 2 a.m. right now as I write this, and I might be just a little loopy. But this is true enough: If you understand exactly what your grass needs, and you feed the grass only when it needs it – instead of fertilizing when it's convenient for you – then you'll have a healthier lawn and grass that looks very good.

Plants need about 16 different elements to keep healthy and grow. Some are easily pulled from the air and water, such as hydrogen, oxygen, and carbon. But a lot of them are not as easy to find – and that's where *you* come in.

The main nutrients plants need – the big three – are

Nitrogen (N), Phosphorus (P), and Potassium (K). These are in just about any kind of fertilizer you pick up at the store.

Then you have secondary nutrients, which are calcium, magnesium, and sulfur, which are usually in the soil and water already. Actually, it's always good to have a soil test and make adjustments to the soil, so you can help the plants access these nutrients more readily.

Last but not least are the micronutrients, which the plant uses in only trace amounts. These include iron, zinc, manganese, copper, molybdenum, boron, and chlorine. Again, these are often available from the soil, and again, get your soil tested so you can add what the soil needs to help release the nutrients to your plants more readily.

All of the above elements are available in all-purpose fertilizers like Miracle-Gro. But you'll be better off feeding the soil with compost or some kind of organic fertilizer. Build up the soil with organic materials, and the plants will do the work for you.

I highly recommend, in whatever gardening you do, feeding the soil some kind of organic material at least once or twice a year. Humus, compost, manure that's broken down so it smells like good clean compost, or any fertilizer with organic materials (I like Bradfield granular fertilizer for this reason) will feed the small creatures in the soil that increase soil fertility. When you build up the hidden world that lives in the soil, these creatures, ranging from soil-dwelling bacteria to springtails to earthworms, break down the organic material you put into the soil in ways that release the nutrients to the grass roots in a way that's easy for the roots to absorb.

Improving soil health improves the health of your lawn. More on this in a minute.

When choosing any other kind of chemical fertilizer, it's important to remember that you're choosing, in effect, a supplement to your organic material. That is, chemical fertilizers are vitamin supplements, while organic materials are the meat-and-potatoes meal for your grasses.

That said, here's a quick overview of the three main elements, also known as N-P-K, listed on your bags and boxes of fertilizer in a ratio of three numbers.

The best ratios of N-P-K for grasses are around 3-1-2 or 4-1-2. (These ratios basically mean that the fertilizer contains 3% Nitrogen, 1% Phosphorus, and 2% Potassium.)

Nitrogen

Nitrogen is the element that grasses need most, and is often used to make the grass greener. However, too much nitrogen can burn the grass, or cause too much top growth. Too much nitrogen also makes the grass succulent and juicy, which insect pests and diseases love. Use only as much nitrogen as your grass needs – but no more. You want a lean, tough, wiry grass.

Fast-release nitrogen (often urea, ammonium nitrate, or ammonium sulfate) is inexpensive and can be used on cold soils. It provides a very fast greenup. Use this in moderation to avoid burning the grass (this kind of fertilizer has a very high salt content) and to keep your grass from popping up too fast. This form of nitrogen will not stick around for very long. It leaches through the soil and then it's gone.

Remember, too, that super-fast growth isn't healthy for a

plant. When your grass shoots up as a result of too much nitrogen fertilizer, the root growth simply can't keep up. The roots have got to provide water that this new growth demands, so they start growing where they can find water – right at the surface. But you don't want surface roots that broil in the hot summer sun – you want your grass to send their roots deep into the soil. What you end up with instead is a shallow root system that won't be able to support your grass when the summer heat and drought hits.

A slow-release, or controlled-release, form of nitrogen is better. These are more expensive, and work better when the soil has warmed up, but these lead to more uniform grass growth and a slower green-up, both of which are a little easier on the grass.

Slow-release fertilizers are released slowly to the plants, and even through they're more expensive, but they require fewer applications, and you can see the results of this fertilizer for a long time.

Of course, organic forms of nitrogen will not burn the grass and are slow-release, which lasts longer over time.

Organic forms of nitrogen include grass clippings. As you saw in previous chapters, if you leave your clippings on the lawn, you can reduce the nitrogen you have to add back to the yard by 25 percent. If you mow weekly, your clippings will be small and will fall back into the grass very nicely. Obviously, if the clippings are bigger and lie in clumps on the lawn, you'll have to rake them up. A good mulching mower can make all the difference.

Don't worry about thatch – clippings don't cause thatch

because they break down quickly. You should see a slight greenup in the lawn a week after your clippings go into the lawn.

Phosphorus

This element supports root growth in grass, as well as healthy shoot growth. Generally this is present in the soil, if you make a point of improving your soils organically. Phosphorus in fertilizer doesn't travel through the soil speedy-quick the way nitrogen does, so it's best to have it already in the soil.

Potassium

You can think of potassium as the health booster for your grass (and other plants). It helps your grass stand up to drought, heat, cold, and your average wear and tear. Potash is the main source of potassium in fertilizer. In sandy soil, it's a good idea to add a little extra potassium. Overall, you don't need to add this in big amounts – a little dab'll do ya.

When's the Best Time to Fertilize?

It depends, because the answer depends on what kind of grass you have. Cool-season grasses should be fertilized in spring and fall. Warm-season grasses should be fertilized in late spring to early summer.

A good rule of thumb with grasses – it's best to fertilize just before the grass has a time of active growth. That helps the grass, whatever kind it is, to green up for the season and get well established before the worst heat of summer hits.

The best time to fertilize is morning, once the grass is dry. If the grass is wet, the fertilizer could stick to the blades and burn the grass. Once you've finished fertilizing, water the lawn to get the fertilizer off the blades and into the soil.

Fertilize your lawn once or twice a year – cool-season grasses in spring and fall; warm-season grasses in spring, mid-summer, and early fall. Now, if you have a high-maintenance lawn, such as a baseball field, fertilize it once a month. But don't go calling your lawn high-maintenance just so you can go to monthly fertilizing. That's just a bridge too far, guys.

ORGANIC FERTILIZERS FOR LAWNS

Chemical fertilizers are helpful, because I have often saved myself time during spring and summer by watering my plants with Miracle-Gro to give them a little boost. But the organic fertilizers that I put down in fall and winter is what really drives the health of my plants, roses, and grass. Chemical fertilizers are vitamin supplements for plants, but organic fertilizers provide the healthy diet for the plants, plus they create a healthy environment for the roots, as well as for the microorganisms and the small creatures that live in the soil, breaking these materials down so the elements are readily absorbed by the roots.

Organic fertilizers are made from animal wastes (well-rotted manure), plant wastes (compost), or rock powder (greensoil).

Different kinds of organic fertilizers that can be spread on lawns:

Rotted manure

Compost

Milorganite (sludge)
Seaweed
Rock powder
Fish fertilizer

That's the straight, non-brand-name stuff. Generally, though, you can trot out to just about any box store or local garden center or nursery and find a couple of bags of organic fertilizers, both granular or liquid, that you can use.

A good thing you can do for your lawn is, after you put down grass seed in the fall, top-dress with compost (that is, spread a light layer of compost over your lawn). You can also top-dress with compost after your aerate your lawn in fall or spring.

Organic fertilizer doesn't do all the flashy stuff that chemical fertilizers do – it doesn't give you a huge flush of green – but it does all the behind-the-scenes work, the underappreciated work out of sight. And if you haven't used very much organic fertilizer before, it's possible that it's going to take a while to rebuild the soil and revive the microorganism life that needs to flourish for best results. It's a worthwhile endeavor, though, one that increases vitality in your grass.

WATERING THE LAWN

Watering the lawn is a topic that needs a little time devoted to it. If you give your lawn much water, then you create a swamp. Not enough water, and the lawn loses some of its greenness, and during a drought, the lawn goes crispy. (However, if your area has water restrictions during a drought – and many places do – seek out and buy grass that's bred to be more drought resistant for your area. The folks at your local university extension service will give you excellent drought-resistant grasses for your part of the state.)

When I worked as a city horticulturist, somebody set up the sprinkler system at Felix Street Square to water daily. It was high summer, and that might have been okay, except the soil at the park, which was built where a hospital used to stand, consisted of some of the thickest clay I had ever seen outside of a subdivision. Clay soil holds on to water like a magnet. Also, since the soil was plastic clay, the water couldn't percolate into the soil at all. So every time the sprinklers turned on, we'd get gigantic puddles all over the place. I had to keep going in and adjusting the water controls until I found a time early in the morning, once a week, where the I could set the sprinklers to water without drenching any bypassers, while also giving the grass there enough water to do well during a drought. It took a little tweaking, but as Yogi Berra said, "You can observe a lot by just watching."

But I've seen other lawns that were overwatered. Even the lawns that had good soil with good drainage would become squishy during the day due to too much water. Don't take your yard to this extreme. It raises your water bill, and it makes all those fertilizer you've applied leach through the soil quickly. So, the water would basically wash all those elements that your lawn needs into the groundwater, or down deep where the roots can't reach them, and dilutes them too much to be of any use.

The ancient Greek saying, "Everything in moderation," certainly applies here.

How much water does turfgrass need?

All it needs is one to two inches of water every week, including rainfall. That's it. You should water deeply and infrequently. You want this water to go deeply into the soil, so the roots will follow it down. The deep, infrequent waterings will help the roots reach into the soil for water. Deep roots are best for grass, because these roots reach into the cool part of the soil where the summer heat can't reach, and that helps the plant. Also, these roots help the grass withstand drought.

Frequent waterings gives you grass with a root system close to the surface of the ground, where the heat can reach them and drought can pull the moisture from both grass blade and grass root. And a lot of the water you give this grass evaporates before it gets deep into the soil.

In the worst-case scenario, too much water in the soil actually deprives the plant's roots of oxygen. Waterlogged soil will also kill your grass.

The best way to water is, not with an automated system, but by turning it on and off manually. Different soils require vastly different methods. Clay soils will start to puddle before you've given your yard the full amount of water. Sandy soils, on the other hand, will let the water drain away before it's had much effect on the grass! For lawns on extreme soil, you might have to shut off the irrigation system for a while, then turn it back on again to allow the water to percolate into the soil, or to allow the roots to absorb the water as it drains away.

Don't worry, though. Every yard is different, and every soil is different. The best way to learn what your yard needs is to observe it carefully and make notes in your gardening notebook. (In the back of this book, I'll have a sample chapter from my vegetable gardening book in which I talk about this gardening notebook. Keep one. A gardening notebook will be a godsend, whatever kind of outdoor work you do.) Observing your yard, how your grass grows, how the soil responds to watering, etc., is the best medicine for anything.

I will tell you that observation is a learning process, and a lot of times you will have to figure out how things work. That's okay. Not all of us have had a turfgrass management class – and sometimes those of us who have had one, can't remember what we've learned in it. Give me a break, it was an 8 o'clock class. But observation, a willingness to learn, and a willingness to try and figure out a solution – these things will take you far.

Watering PRN – Only As Needed

A lot of sports groundskeepers and turf specialists suggest to water and feed the lawn, not when it's convenient for you, but only when the lawn needs it.

This is where the observation really kicks in – listen to your lawn, and it will tell you want you need to do next.

Obviously it's not going to say, "Hey, Bob, I need some compost. And while you're up, I have some dollar spot forming over here on the right, so could you lighten up on the water and spray a little baking soda solution on the fungus? It's feeling a little itchy there." Though this information would be infinitely helpful from a lawn.

On the other hand, if lawns talked, you'd probably hear a lot of homeowners crying, "My lawn talks and it won't shut up about the benefits of organic fertilizers!" Well, there's a reason for that.

Anyway, listening to your lawn is just observing, as always. But the best time to water is when your lawn asks.

Keep an eye on your yard for signs of stress. The grass might turn a bluish color with a slightly wilted look. Also, look for signs of "footprinting" – that is, when you walk across the grass and leave footprints that don't spring back quickly.

That's when you need to water the grass deeply.

The amount of wilt you see in the grass will be different every week, due to different weather stresses, amount of rainfall, humidity, windiness, humidity, etc. But if you let your lawn tell you when it's ready to water, you get a healthier lawn, and you use less water (which is great if you live in a place where water rationing is mandatory).

A lawn in summer will go dormant and look a little yellow. This also is normal. You can allow your lawn to be yellowish until it rains again, though it's unattractive. If you water the lawn during its dormant phase, you'll end up using more water. And some places have water restrictions, so allowing your lawn to go dormant will have to be the norm. Once the restrictions are over, it will take several waterings or thunderstorms to get the grass to green back up. If you see areas in your yard that don't recover, find a grass variety that is more drought-tolerant and seed those areas with that.

The best time to water.

For best results, water in the morning. In the cool of the morning, water is less likely to evaporate away, and the lawn has plenty of time to dry out before evening. Evening waterings can be bad for lawns, because the moisture that lingers among the grass blades in the coolness can lead to fungal diseases. If you water in the middle of the day in the heat, you can lose up to 30 to 40 percent of your water to evaporation before it can soak into the root zone. (However, if the grass is stressed due to heat, sometimes I'll give it a quick watering to help cool it off a bit. Really, that watering probably helps me more than it helps the grass.)

A. BLANC.

ENGRAVER
FOR FLORISTS & NURSERYMEN.
ELECTROTYPES. CHEAP

Parties about to issue catalogues, and those requiring engravings and electros, should send for list of cuts Illustrated. Prices reduced. Cuts for catalogue covers cheaper than type. Ornamental cuts for advertisements, bill heads, note heads, envelopes, seed bags, &c. If you have prints of any cut you want, send them for estimate. Electrotyping done promptly and cheaply.

A. BLANC, 314 N. 11th St., PHILADELPHIA, PA.

f.12

This isn't actually lawn-related, but I liked this because the illustrations in this book were drawn by people like A. Blanc above, so I got a little kick out of this "behind the scenes" view of the illustrators who drew those old pictures.

MOWING THE YARD

When it comes down to it, the bulk of your lawn maintenance work is going to be spent on mowing. It's also the best way to keep down the weeds and keep the grass looking good. So it's worth doing your mowing right.

Here's one important thing to remember, though. When you cut your grass, its roots stop growing. True story. This limits the grass's ability to absorb water and elements from the soil. Also, the grass has to make up for photosynthesis lost from the top of the blade, which has been cut off. The grass starts producing new plants from the crown while growing back its top. These new plants make your lawn denser – which is exactly what you want from grass.

Fun plant fact: Any time you stress a plant, it's going to start trying to reproduce itself. If you don't water your houseplant, it thinks "Oh no I'm going to die!" and it starts flowering with an eye toward propagating itself before it croaks. Grass does the same thing when low water spurs it to put out new plants.

Of course, there's a point where you stress the grass or your houseplant so much that it runs out of stored resources (carbohydrates, sugars, etc.) and it can't propagate itself, and then it really *does* die. But a mild stressor such as cutting (which turfgrass is bred to put up with anyway) simply spurs it on to self-propagate. You're welcome.

Here's another rule of thumb that also applies to all plants, from grass to perennials to shrubs to trees: Don't cut off more than a third of a plant. So, when you're mowing, don't cut off more than a third of the grass blade.

There are times, however, when you can't keep up with the mowing. Then your grass will need to be cut by over a third to get close to a normal height. These things happen. In the initial mowing, cut the grass as high as possible. Then bring it down to its normal height in the next mowing.

Really, grass should generally be cut low in seasons when it's actively growing, and then high in summer when it's hot, or when it's stressed. Obviously some grass in special situations (such as putting greens) should always be cut short. Certain kinds of grasses, such as bentgrass, also need to be cut short, or else they flop over.

Don't cut the grass too short, especially in summer. If you leave bare patches in your yard, then weeds and crabgrass have a place to grow up and are able to get a foothold in your yard. Keep your grass mowed high in summer, to shade the ground, to keep weed seeds from getting a foothold, and to hold in a little moisture.

Cutting your grass high also allows your turfgrass to grow longer roots. You remember how cutting grass puts its root system growth on pause? Consistently cutting your grass shorter than its recommended height also shortens its root system. Cut the grass high so the root system is vigorous – you want those deep roots on your grass for a vigorous lawn.

How often should you mow?

Going back to the One-Third rule, i.e. "Try not to remove more than one-third of the total leaf surface of your grass," that would mean cutting your grass every four to five days when it's rapidly growing (usually in spring), and then less frequently in summer as its growth slows due to the summer heat.

So, about every week – more often when the grass is growing quickly, less often when the growth slows.

The nice thing about the one-third rule is that this more frequent mowing will give you short clippings that won't clump on your lawn, allowing you to recycle those clippings into the yard – organic fertilizer for your grass.

The best time to mow

Yesterday we had the total eclipse. I live right in the line of totality, and it would have been a very neat experience, except for all those thick clouds hiding the sun. And the light drizzle that was falling on us. And, to top off the whole experience, my neighbor across the street got this goofball idea to mow his lawn through the whole eclipse – even when the light disappeared and it was dark as early night outside! NOT THE TIME TO MOW, MISTER. People are weird.

So okay, don't mow during a total eclipse in the rain. Most of the time, this is not going to be a thing, obviously.

The best time to mow in the summer – in the cool of the early evening, about 6 to 7 p.m. The grass is dry, the heat of the day has eased up by this time, and there's still enough light to see by so you're not mowing in the dark, like some goofballs. Mowing during the day in the summer heat – why do that?

Actually, try to avoid it when you can. One August when temperatures were hovering at 95 to 100 degrees for the full month, a man died because he was mowing his yard in 95 degree heat. That's an extreme example – I'm sure you're not going to do that – but if you have to work in the heat, make sure you take water breaks. If you start feeling dizzy or lightheaded, stop what you're doing and get into the shade. Heat stroke and heat exhaustion are serious matters.

GET SHARP – QUICK TIPS ABOUT MOWING

It's actually more beneficial to your lawn if you mow when the grass needs it, instead of at the same time every week. Of course, this isn't the easiest thing to do – we have lives, too, you know! – but if you eye your lawn and see it getting ragged, and you have the time, get 'er done.

Look at the optimal mowing height for whichever grass makes up the majority of your lawn. Then do some math to figure out how tall the grass can get, remembering the One-Third rule, before it's time to mow. So if your lawn is mostly Kentucky bluegrass, which does best at 3 inches in summer, you should cut the grass by the time it hits 4 ½ inches (or before), to avoid cutting off more than a third of the blade. Get into the practice of eyeing how tall your grass should be compared to your shoe as you stand in it. Then you know that if your grass is over the top of your shoe, it's time to fire up the mower.

Keep your mower's blades clean and sharp. If the blades are dull, they won't cut grass but tear it. (A ragged cut won't heal as quickly as a clean cut, which allows diseases into the grass, something you don't need!)

You can tell if your blade is dull by looking at the top of your grass blades. A sharpened blade will leave the top of the grass with a nice clean cut. A dull blade will leave a ragged tear at the top.

You can sharpen the blade yourself by putting it in a vise and sharpening the beveled edge with a file, then put it on a cone level to see if the blade is balanced. If it isn't, put it back in the vise and file a little bit more off the heavy side, and keep checking the blade until it's balanced. Or, you can have the blade professionally sharpened.

Before you mow, pick up sticks around the yard, because running over a stick is a hazard to you, and it dulls that nice sharp blade you just fixed up.

Make sure your blade is at the right height before you start mowing. I found this out the hard way once when I borrowed my grandpa's mower and forgot to adjust the mowing deck and absolutely scalped the heck out of part of my front yard. Have you ever seen a little kid who's given himself a haircut?

That was what my yard looked like. Like the little kid, my lawn finally grew back out, but it took a little while.

If you do have a mishap where you mow too low, here's something that will help the poor grass recover. Water the grass with a fertilizer that includes the trace minerals calcium, manganese, and iron. Then give the grass a deep morning watering. Then give it a little extra water as it grows back for the next couple of weeks.

Don't mow when it's wet. Clumps of grass will gum up the inside of your mower, and clumps of grass clippings will lie on top of your newly-mowed grass. Whatever you do, it's just a mess. Wait for things to dry out a little before you get the mower out.

Mow in the early evening – not in the heat of the day. The grass is already stressed by the heat. Mowing it only adds to its distress. And the root system that it needs to recover from the heat will also be curtailed by the mowing. That's why early evening mowing is best, because the grass can have all night to recover in the coolness and the dark before the sun comes out again.

Slopes are tricky. Mowing across them or mowing straight up and down them can be hard to do. Try to mow them on the diagonal.

When you're done mowing, take a moment to hose down the blade and the deck to get all the grass out of there. Check the blades to be sure they're still looking good, and make any quick fixes if they need them.

How to Winterize Your Lawn Mower

Once the frost hit, it's time to pull the mower into the garage and get it ready for its long winter's nap.

Gas shouldn't stay in the mower over the winter because it could jell and clog the carburetor. Run the mower until it completely runs out of gas. Or, you could add a fuel stabilizer to the gas in the tank if there's too much to waste in that way. After adding the stabilizer, run the mower for about five minutes to get the mixed gas through the machine.

Change the oil and filter on the mower so it's ready to go next spring. Also, this gives you a chance to check for contaminants in the system, if you know what you're looking for.

Clean up all parts of the mower. Have the blades sharpened and balanced. Clean out the deck while the blades are out, and all parts above deck, too, then set it out in the sun so it dries completely. Do the same for the bag that collects clippings.

Tighten all nuts and bolts, and check all belts, safety shields, and filters. Spray all steel parts, including the blade, with penetrating oil.

If you have a reel mower, have a professional sharpen the blades on it.

Finally, store the mower in a dry place out of the rain. If you must store it outside, cover it securely with a waterproof tarp.

First, your lawn mower.

• Siphon the gas out of the mower, and put that into your car. Then you won't have gas clogging up the carburetor. Or you can add some fuel stabilizer. Run the mower for five minutes after adding it.

• Oil the blades to protect them from rust. Finally, disconnect the spark plug and give the mower an oil change.

Nice pants!

LAWN MAINTENANCE IN SPRING

It's spring at last! Rake away the heavy, wet leaves from last year, but don't rake so vigorously that you take all the new grass with them.

Sow grass seed, covering it with straw mulch to protect it from erosion and drying winds. Try not to let the grass seed dry out. You may have to keep running outside with the sprinkler to keep up with the drying effects of sun and wind on pleasant days.

If you have an established yard, raise the mowing height for bluegrass and fescues to 3 inches. For heaven's sake, don't scalp the lawn. Scalping is when one cuts the grass so low that only nubs are left. If dust is flying into the air as you mow, you're scalping. This is a bad practice because grass that's scalped is severely stressed -- one shouldn't remove more than the top third of the grass while mowing.

And once the forest of grass blades no longer shades the ground, weed seeds are able to germinate. Since weeds grow faster than grass, there will be a nice crop of dandelions the next time you come out to mow.

Cutting the grass too low also curtails its rooting system. A taller grass will have a more extensive root system than grass that has been cut down to little nubs. Shallow roots means a faster drying-out time when the summer heat hits.

Taller grass allows the lawn to shade itself: the roots stay cool, the growth shades out weeds, and less water is needed on the lawn. There's also more leaf surface on the grass, which means more photosynthesis -- greater food production. It means better health overall for the lawn.

That's also why it's a good idea to let the grass clippings fall into the lawn instead of raking them up or bagging them (but do rake them out if the clippings clump on the yard).

University extensions centers are encouraging homeowners to stop bagging grass clippings. Instead, they should let their grass clippings fall back into the grass.

Many think that grass clippings cause thatch. However, that is not the case. Thatch is actually a mat of grass roots and creeping runners -- not clippings. Grass clippings are 75 to 80 percent water. Once the clipped grass withers, which doesn't take long, the remaining bit of grass decomposes quickly. To see for yourself, leave some clippings on your garden border, and watch them for a week or two.

Clippings acts as a light mulch, which keeps grass from drying out, shades out weed seeds and keeps thatch from accumulating in the first place. And keeping the clippings on your yard saves on landfill space – and saves you time.

The benefits don't end there. When you let the clips fall where they may, you can use 20 to 25 percent less fertilizer on your yard. This is because clippings contain 4 percent nitrogen, 1 percent phosphorus and 3 percent potassium, as well as trace minerals.

A layer of clippings also encourages earthworms. They in turn create a healthier soil layer -- their tunneling creates air space in the soil, which the roots need, and earthworm castings are rich food for grass. (You can actually buy earthworm castings, but they are expensive.)

Finally, don't go overboard with the fertilizer. Nitrogen is good on the lawn, but too much of it will make the grass juicy and sweet for insect pests. Also, it makes for lawn-cutting nightmares. Follow label requirements to the letter.

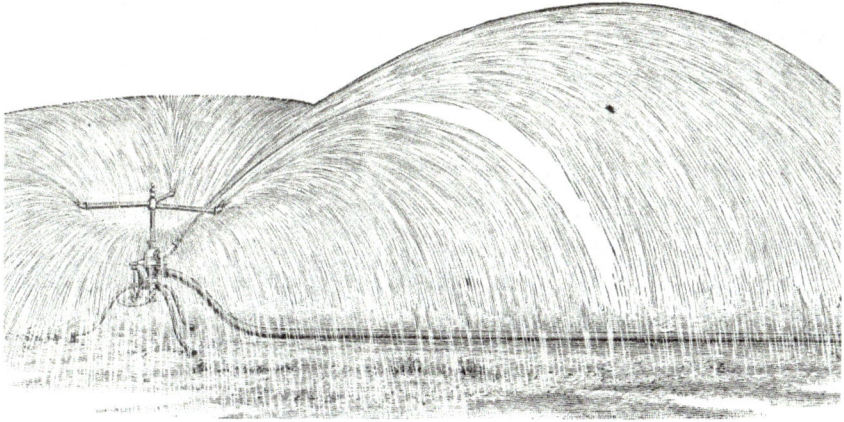

LAWN MAINTENANCE IN SUMMER

Hot weather, kids out playing, and guys who scalp the lawn with Weed-Eaters can really do a number on lawns. Help your yard through the rest of the summer with these tips.

First of all, mowing. Disconnect the spark plug from your mower, then turn the mower over to look at the blades. One of the biggest causes of grass problems is dull blades, which tear the grass rather than cut it, leaving frayed edges that take longer to heal than smooth cuts.

Sharpen blades once a month, or after eight hours of mowing, for optimal performance. Take the blades to a professional sharpener. If you want to sharpen them yourself, keep that spark plug disconnected, remove the blade and set it in a vise, then sharpen to the original cutting angle. File equal amounts from both ends to keep the blades balanced.

Raise the mowing height for bluegrass and fescues to 3 inches. Grass that's tall and thick will keep moisture from escaping and will allow the roots to stay cool. That's also why it's a good idea to let the grass clippings fall into the lawn instead of raking them up (but do rake them up if they clump on the yard). The clippings act as mulch, releasing nutrients back into the soil.

Scalping is when one cuts the grass so low that only nubs are left. Once the grass blades no longer shades the ground, weed seeds are able to germinate. Also, a tall blade of grass will have a more extensive root system than one that has been cut down to a nub. Shallow roots means a faster drying-out time when the heat hits.

Reduce the amount of nitrogen you feed the grass, or even stop giving your yard nitrogen altogether. Nitrogen makes a grass succulent and soft, and what you want is a lean, mean grass to get through this hot weather. If you fertilize, increase the amount of potassium you give it instead.

Instead of sprinkling chemicals on the grass, feed the grass compost instead. Once a month, scatter a layer of compost over the grass with a spreader or by hand. Compost is super plant food that discourages thatch and adds beneficial micronutrients to the soil, and it suppresses fungal diseases. Worms like it, too. Happy worms equal a healthy soil. (Also, if you get enough activity with worms and other good critters in the soil, they'll help aerate the soil all through the growing season.)

Instead of "feeding" the lawn with chemicals that do

nothing to improve the soil, use organic lawn food instead. Spraying the lawn with seaweed extract helps the grass fight heat stress. Fish emulsion and bone meal is also good. Corn gluten meal will keep weed seeds from germinating and adds nitrogen to the soil.

Watering is another way to help the yard. One inch of moisture every week, if it doesn't rain, will give the grass all the water it needs. Water a little extra near buildings and other heat-reflecting surfaces.

Take care not to over-water, especially if the yard is poorly drained or if the soil consists of heavy clay. Over-watering can lead to drowned roots and outbreaks of fungal diseases. Give the grass an inch of water every week. Water early in the morning twice a week for best results. To water during the day or evening invites disease.

A vintage lawnmower -- so lightweight that even a child could use it!

PREVIEWS OF MY OTHER GARDENING BOOKS

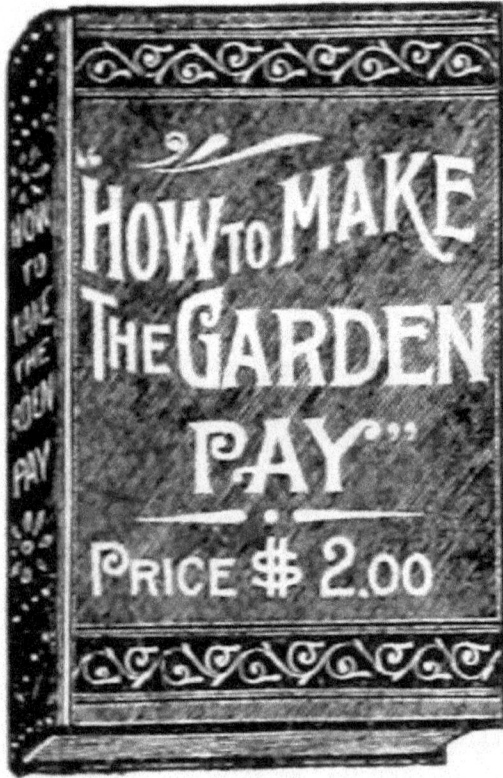

Don't Throw in the Trowel: Vegetable Gardening Month by Month.

A sample!

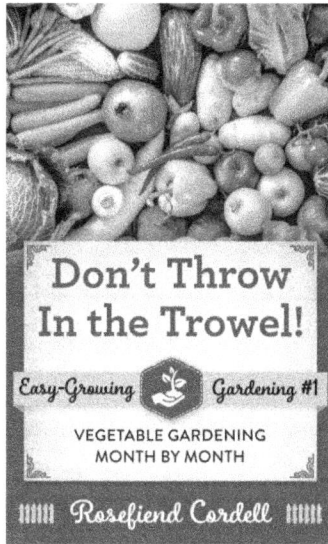

Two things:

First: You know more about gardening than you think.

Second: A garden – the soil – plants – all of these are very forgiving. When it comes down to it, you can make a lot of mistakes and still come out with good results.

***Don't Throw in the Trowel! Vegetable Gardening Month by Month** includes info on seeds, transplanting, growing, and harvesting, as well as diseases, garden pests, and organic gardening. I also talk about garden prep, because a good plan, a garden notebook, and a little off-season work will save you a lot of trouble down the road.*

I've worked in horticulture for 20 years: in landscape design and installation, as a greenhouse tech, perennials manager, and city horticulturist & rosarian. This book shares what I've learned so far.

JANUARY

Save Time and Trouble With Garden Journals

When I worked as a municipal horticulturist, I took care of twelve high-maintenance gardens, and a number of smaller ones, over I-don't-know-how-many square miles of city, plus several hundred small trees, an insane number of shrubs, a greenhouse, and whatever else the bosses threw at me. I had to find a way to stay organized besides waking up at 3 a.m. to make extensive lists. My solution: keep a garden journal.

Vegetable gardeners with an organized journal can take control of production and yields. Whether you have a large garden or a small organic farm, it certainly helps to keep track of everything in order to beat the pests, make the most of your harvest, and keep up with spraying and fertilizing.

Keeping a garden journal reduces stress because your overtaxed brain won't have to carry around all those lists. It saves time by keeping you focused. Writing sharpens the mind, helps it to retain more information, and opens your eyes to the world around you.

My journal is a small five-section notebook, college ruled, and I leave it open to the page I'm working on at the time. The only drawback with a spiral notebook is that after a season or two I have to thumb through a lot of pages to find an earlier comment. A small three-ring binder with five separators would do the trick, too. If you wish, you can take out pages at the end of each season and file them in a master notebook.

I keep two notebooks – one for ornamentals and one for vegetables. However, you might prefer to pile everything into one notebook. Do what feels comfortable to you.

These are the five sections I divide my notebooks into – though you might use different classifications, or put them in different orders. Don't sweat it; this ain't brain surgery. Feel free to experiment. You'll eventually settle into the form that suits you best.

First section: To-do lists.

This is pretty self-explanatory: you write a list, you cross off almost everything on it, you make a new list.

When I worked as horticulturist, I did these lists every month. I'd visit all the gardens I took care of. After looking at anything left unfinished on the previous month's list, and looking at the garden to see what else needed to be done, I made a new, comprehensive list.

Use one page of the to-do section for reminders of things you need to do next season. If it's summer, and you think of some chores you'll need to do this fall, make a FALL page and write them down. Doing this has saved me lots of headaches.

Second section: Reference lists.

These are lists that you'll refer back to on occasion.

For example, I'd keep a list of all the yews in the parks system that needed trimmed, a list of all gardens that needed weekly waterings, a list of all places that needed sprayed for bagworms, a list of all the roses that needed to be babied, etc.

I would also keep my running lists in this section, too – lists I keep adding to.

For instance, I kept a list of when different vegetables were ready for harvest – even vegetables I didn't grow, as my friends and relatives reported to me. Then when I made a plan for my veggie garden, I would look at the list to get an idea of when these plants finished up, and then I could figure out when I could take them out and put in a new crop. I also had a list of "seed-to-harvest" times, so I could give each crop enough time to make the harvest date before frost.

You can also keep a wish list – plants and vegetables you'd like to have in your garden.

Third section: Tracking progress.

This is a weekly (or, "whenever it occurs to me to write about it") section as well.

If you plant seeds in a greenhouse, keep track of what seeds you order, when you plant them, when they germinate, how many plants you transplant (and how many survive to maturity), and so forth.

When you finish up in the greenhouse, use these pages to look back and record your thoughts – "I will never again try to start vinca from seeds! Never!! Never!!!" Then you don't annoy yourself by forgetting and buying vinca seeds next year.

You can do the same thing when you move on to the vegetable garden – what dates you tilled the ground, planted the seeds, when they germinated, and so forth. Make notes on yields and how everything tasted. "The yellow crooknecks were definitely not what I'd hoped for. Try yellow zucchini next year."

Be sure to write a vegetable garden overview at season's end, too. "Next year, for goodness' sake, get some 8-foot poles for the beans! Also, drive the poles deeper into the ground so they don't fall over during thunderstorms."

During the winter, you can look back on this section and see ways you can improve your yields and harvest ("The dehydrator worked great on the apples!"), and you can see which of your experiments worked.

Fourth section: Details of the natural world.

When keeping a journal, don't limit yourself to what's going on in your garden. Track events in the natural world, too. Write down when the poplars start shedding cotton or when the Queen's Anne Lace blooms.

You've heard old gardening maxims such as "plant corn when oak leaves are the size of a squirrel's ear," or "prune roses when the forsythia blooms." If the spring has been especially cold and everything's behind, you can rely on nature's cues instead of a calendar when planting or preventing disease outbreaks.

Also, by setting down specific events, you can look at the journal later and say, "Oh, I can expect little caterpillars to attack the indigo plant when the Johnson's Blue geranium is blooming." Then next year, when you notice the buds on your geraniums, you can seek out the caterpillar eggs and squish them before they hatch. An ounce of prevention, see?

When I read back over this section of the journal, patterns start to emerge. I noticed that Stargazer lilies bloom just as the major heat begins. This is no mere coincidence: It's happened for the last three years! So now when I see the large buds, I give the air conditioner a quick checkup.

Fifth section: Notes and comments.

This is more like the journal that most people think of as being a journal – here, you just talk about the garden, mull over how things are looking, or grouse about those supposedly blight-resistant tomatoes that decided to be contrary and keel over from blight.

I generally put a date on each entry, then ramble on about any old thing. You can write a description of the garden at sunset, sketch your peppers, or keep track of the habits of bugs you see crawling around in the plants. This ain't art, this is just fun stuff (which, in the end, yields great dividends).

Maybe you've been to a garden talk on the habits of Asian melons and you need a place to put your notes. Put them here!

This is a good place to put garden plans, too. Years later I run into them again, see old mistakes I've made, and remember neat ideas I haven't tried yet.

Get a calendar.

Then, when December comes, get next year's calendar and the

gardening journal and sit down at the kitchen table. Using last year's notes, mark on the calendar events to watch out for -- when the tomatoes first ripen, when the summer heat starts to break, and when you expect certain insects to attack. In the upcoming year, you just look at the calendar and say, "Well, the squash bugs will be hatching soon," so you put on your garden gloves and start smashing the little rafts of red eggs on the plants.

A garden journal can be a fount of information, a source of memories, and most of all, a way to keep organized. Who thought a little spiral notebook could do so much?

If you enjoy this book, grab a copy at your favorite retailer!

Rose to the Occasion: An Easy-Growing Guide to Rose Gardening

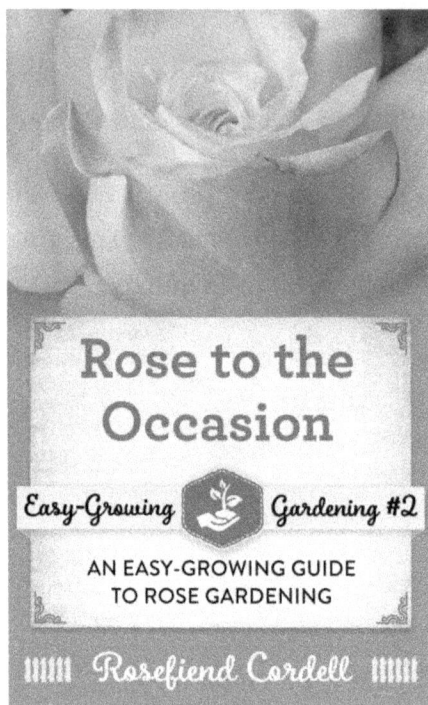

Roses are the Queen of Flowers. They're beautiful, fragrant, and elegant - and roses require all the pampering of a real Queen, don't they?

Actually, they don't!

Rose gardening can be easy and pleasant. I've worked 25 years in horticulture and cared for over 300 roses in a public rose garden when I was municipal horticulturist. I found ways to keep rose gardening fussbudgetry to a minimum while growing vigorous roses that bloomed their heads off. Rose to the Occasion: An Easy-Growing Guide to Rose Gardening shares tricks and shortcuts that rosarians use, plus simple ways you can keep up with your to-do list in the rose garden.

Gardeners of all skill levels will find this book helpful, whether they be beginning gardeners or old rosarians, whether they have a green thumb or a brown thumb.

Rose to the Occasion is the ultimate resource for any rose gardener, or anybody in need of good gardening advice. Roses are filled with romance, history, color, and fragrance. Grow some. They are worth it.

INTRODUCTION

When I started working as city horticulturist, I took care of a bunch of gardens around the city, including the big Krug Park rose garden. It included a bunch of the usual scrawny tea roses, some shrub roses, and a bunch of bare ground.

At the time I was more of a perennials gal, but when I looked at the roses, some of them were really nice. The 'Carefree Delight' roses were covered with rumpled pink blossoms. There was a tall 'Mr. Lincoln' rose and some 'Double Delights' that smelled amazing. A bunch of 'Scarlet Meidilands' were really putting on a blooming show, with tiny scarlet flowers cascading all over them. Not shabby at all.

I started taking care of the roses, but I noticed that a lot of the 'Scarlet Meidilands' were sprouting odd growths. Most of the new growth looked fine, with bronzed, flat leaves that looked attractive. But some of the new growth was markedly different – skinny, stunted leaves with pebbled surfaces, and hyperthorny canes that were downright rubbery. The blossoms on these shoots were crinkled and didn't open worth a darn.

I hollered at Charles Anctil, a Master Rosarian with the American Rose Society. We'd known each other since 1992 when we both worked at the Old Mill Nursery. He'd been working with roses for a good 50 years, and he knows his stuff. At any rate, Charles looked over the roses and told me that those roses, and others, had rose rosette virus, a highly contagious disease, and a death sentence for a rose. Every one of those roses had to come out. He couldn't believe the extent of the damage. He said that he had never seen so many roses infected by rose rosette in one place.

Oh great! Why do I get to be the lucky one?

I dug up many roses that spring. That winter, I got a work crew and dug up 50 more. I had to replace all those roses, so I started researching new varieties.

As city horticulturist with no staff, I was already running like hell everywhere I went, so I wanted roses that wouldn't wilt or croak or wrap themselves in blackspot every time I looked at them cross-eyed. I wanted tough roses, roses that took heat and drought and bug attacks and zombie apocalypses with aplomb and would still come out looking great and covered with scented blossoms. (And the blossoms HAD to be scented – there was no two ways about that.)

I started reading rose catalogs. I talked to Charles some more, which is always fun. Somewhere along the way, I got obsessed. I immersed myself in roses. That's how I learn – I get excited about a subject and start reading everything in sight about it, as if it's a mini-course in school. I read about antique roses, which were making a comeback. Different rose breeders, most notably David Austin, were crossing modern varieties with old varieties and to get roses that combined the best of the new and the old. Other breeders were creating roses that were tough and disease-resistant, such as the 'Knock-Out' landscape rose, which now you see everywhere.

I planted some antique roses, and they looked great. I planted more. The rose garden was starting to look spiffy, even though I still had to take roses out every year due to the rose rosette virus. I even tucked in some annuals and perennials around the garden to doll up the place when the roses conked out in July and August.

Roses are amazing plants. Many old roses have a long and storied history. Some species that were growing during the time of the Pyramids are still blooming today. And these roses are attractive and fragrant. What could be better?

Some people say that you can't grow roses organically. I say you can. I did use a few chemicals when I was a horticulturist, but that was because I had a huge list of things to do in a limited amount of time. I used Round Up for spot-weeding (a tiny squirt for each weed, just enough to wet the leaves), a systemic granular fungicide to keep up with blackspot, and Miracle-Gro as part of the fertilizing regimen for convenience.

If you choose to use chemicals, use them responsibly. Don't spray them and expect the problem to be fixed. They work best when you combine them with other control methods. I'll give you an example that's not rose-related. I had a mandevilla plant in the greenhouse

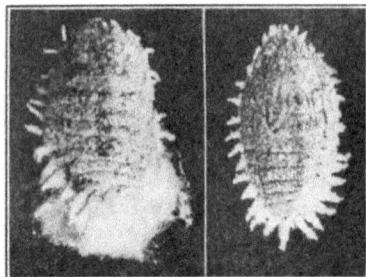

that had a huge mealybug problem. (Mealybugs are a small, white insect that sucks out plant juices. The young bugs look like bits of cotton.) I sprayed the plant with insecticide until the leaves were dripping. The mealybugs were still there. I put a systemic insecticide around the roots of the plant and watered it in. The mealybugs didn't care.

So I just started squishing the mealybugs with my fingers, a gross job because they squirt orange goo. At that point, I didn't care. I searched them out and squashed them where they were cuddled up around buds, in the cracks of the plant, and under the leaves. I even found some on the roots just under the soil. I squished those and added a little extra potting soil. I checked the plant every other day and squished every mealybug I could find. After a while, I stopped finding them altogether. Then I fertilized the plant, and the mandevilla put out leaves like crazy and started blooming. Success!

Chemicals aren't a cure-all by any means. They're convenient, but sometimes you just have to get in and do a little hands-on work with the plant to help it along. It's a good feeling when a plant you've been working with rights itself and perks up again.

Though I'm no longer a horticulturist, I wrote this book because I have worked in horticulture for about half my life, and have a decent understanding about how the natural world works. I might possibly be just a little crazy about roses. I hope my experiences are helpful and that you're able to benefit from them – and that your roses benefit as well.

The end of the sample!!

If you like this chapter, you can find the whole ebook or paperback of Rose to the Occasion at your favorite retailer.

Perennial Classics: Planting & Growing Great Perennial Gardens

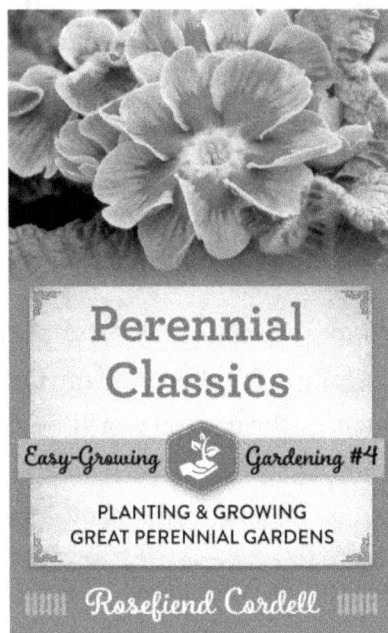

INTRODUCTION

WHY ARE PERENNIALS HARD TO BEAT?

When I was in college, I hit a rough patch and had to drop out. I was working two part-time jobs while taking full-time classes, paying for rent, food, and college (I had no financial aid), while living on ramen and hot dogs. (Fun fact: Due to my poverty diet, the iron levels in my blood were so low that I was not allowed to give blood.) Also, I kept wanting to change majors – I wanted to be an English major, but I kept being told that I needed to get a major that I could earn money in. "You can't make a living out of writing books." So I came back home and started living in my old hometown of

Nodaway, and I got a job at a garden center.

I had a great boss and co-workers at the garden center. We worked with the annuals, perennials, and herbs. We would sing while grooming the plants (when I say "grooming the plants," I mean picking the dead leaves and old flowers off the plants – we weren't brushing the plants' hair or anything). We had a lot of good stuff to talk about, and we helped customers find what they wanted, and when they had gardening questions and we didn't know the answers, we'd do everything we could to find the answer. It was a great deal.

The nice thing about working at a garden center is that you get a lot of free plants. Every day you'd work through the flats and pots, and if you saw any plants that were dying or droopy or looked bad, you'd take them out. Some of them just needed a little tender loving care, so those would go to the "plant hospital," as we called it, where they would get a little attention and to perk up. Some of these would recover enough to go back on the tables, but some just sat there looking mopey, so we got to take these home.

I had a bit of a garden where I lived, but now I had a lot of garden. I wasn't very interested in annuals, because they were there for a season and that was it for them. But I loved the perennials. After all these years, I'm trying to put my finger on why they appealed so much to me. I think it was because everybody grew the same annuals over and over – marigolds, geraniums, petunias – but perennials weren't as common. I always go for stuff that's a little uncommon.

Another part of it was that some of these perennials could be true heirlooms in the garden, growing for years and years. I really wanted to grow a Gas Plant (*Dictamnus albus*) because they could stay alive for decades. Alas, the ones we had were just not in very good shape, and I didn't have much luck getting them started in my garden.

At the time, too, I was a little tired of the sameness of all the annuals. Granted, I would change my mind later, when I was working as a city horticulturist, because annuals were such a help in coloring up my flower beds fast. But give me a break, I was in college, and at that time I was just a teeny bit pretentious. Okay, more than a teeny bit.

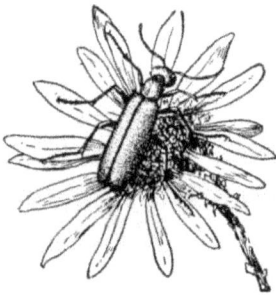

ASTERS

Blister Beetles: The black is the most common; it feeds upon the flowers. Daily hunting and shaking the beetles into a pan of kerosene will quickly

I also loved the variety of perennials. I had some Connecticut Blue delphiniums that bloomed in the most gorgeous shades of blue I'd ever seen in a plant. I had a Japanese anemone that was a whirligig of white flowers until a bunch of blister beetles ate it up. The jerks. Sea thrift, with its little powder-puff flowers growing out of a tuft of grass; Nepeta, or catmint, with its purple flowers. My cat was nuts about catnip, but she had no interest whatsoever in catmint. I planted some dahlia tubers and got some fascinating, gigantic flowers. A perennial hibiscus startled me with magenta flowers as big as dinner plates. Grandma Mary wanted to know what these plants were! And she is wise in all things plant, so that's saying something.

Now, bringing home a bunch of random plants from the nursery doesn't exactly make for an orderly garden. But I didn't care. I loved most the anticipation – of putting this sad, sickly little plant in the ground and giving it good soil and watering it regularly, and generally the plant would perk up and start growing, and the next year it would start flowering, and whoa! So that's what the flowers look like in real life! And it all started with a sad-looking little droopy twig.

That's one of the really cool things about perennials. They can fill a number of roles in the garden. You can get them in a variety of shapes, forms, and colors – whether they're chunky or elegant, variegated or colorful leaves, sprawling stems or upright, billowing and carefree or architecturally perfect. Perennials grow in all kinds of conditions, whether it's shade, desert, heat, or cold, and build the background of beautiful borders. Perennials can provide four-season beauty, and they grow stronger by the season. Perennials promise all these things – and they deliver.

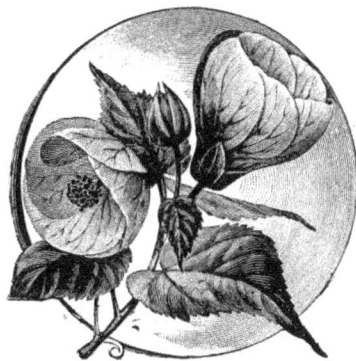

At the end of the spring season, when things were slowing down, I was hanging around the garden center one day with my boss and co-worker, just talking. I said, "You know what? I think I'm going to go back to school. And this time, I'm going to major in horticulture. You guys want to come with me?"

"Sure!" they said.

We ended up commuting to school together and took horticulture classes together, and I finally graduated four years later, or close enough. (I minored in writing, naturally.) So, again, perennials turned out to be very helpful. I did my senior thesis on English gardens and totally snowed my Senior Studies professor. He was an Ag man who didn't know much about gardening, so I got an A.

Shortly thereafter, I got a job as city horticulturist. I had a million gardens to plant in the spring. I planted annuals everywhere, but boy, that repetitive motion really hurt my hands and wrists. I used a trowel. Then I tried using bulb planters, which were not effective in the clayey soils in city gardens. Finally I used a little child's shovel to dig a series of holes, then dropped the annuals in and covered them up, in order to save my hands and wrists from all that digging. But this was a lot of labor in spring, and I was always so far behind on all the tasks that needed tending to.

So that fall, I bought a bunch of cheap perennials (everything goes on sale in the fall), wrote down the colors and blooming times for them so I could sort out what would look best where, and then I put them in various gardens to fill out the borders. A one-time planting saved a lot of time and trouble in the spring. Once the perennials filled out and started doing their thing, I didn't have to plant so many annuals, which eased my workload. Now I could do all the other things that needed done, which I couldn't do before because I had been planting annuals.

Oh, and I was a one-woman crew for the whole city. I was assigned inmate labor, but I couldn't send them off by themselves to work on other gardens – too bad. Or I'd get somebody doing community service, which was more of a babysitting job – decidedly unhelpful! At least in the summer I had a very helpful seasonal worker, and how I wish I could have had her working with me in early spring and early fall. But you can't have everything, I suppose.

I had perennials going in everywhere, even in the rose garden, for extra color and to give me an easier time in general. The nice thing was, in fall I could divide the perennials, then plant them out and have many more perennials. I could gather the seeds in October and November, when I was cleaning up the gardens, and plant them in the greenhouse to spread around the parks next spring. Your taxpayer dollars at work.

Anyway, this is why I am such a big fan of perennials. In recent years, roses have pretty much eclipsed perennials for me, These days, I'm starting to come back around to perennials again. They're easy to take care of, they offer a multitude of forms and shapes and sizes and colors and blooming times, and once they're in the ground, they're pretty good about growing for a long time. They got me into my major in college (finally), they saved me a lot of time as a horticulturist, and they look good. All in all, a very, very helpful kind of plant to have.

This book will show you around this fascinating world of perennials. I'll show you how to figure out what you need in your garden by looking at what your garden has to offer your plants in terms of site, the amount of sunlight and rain it gets, and ways to improve the soil for best results. I'll talk about garden design (because with perennials, you work with not only color, but coordinating bloom times for all-season color), how to care for your perennials, how to keep them looking good through the year, and ways to troubleshoot your garden problems, whether it's insect pests, diseases, animals, or weeds.

Welcome aboard!

Me in 1995, when I embarked upon the grand adventure
of being a published author.
I was kind of a writing hotshot back then.
If you want to be perfectly honest, I still am.

ABOUT THE AUTHOR

I've worked in most all aspects of horticulture – garden centers, wholesale greenhouses, as a landscape designer, and finally as city horticulturist, where I took care of 20+ gardens around the city. I live in northwest Missouri with my husband and kids, the best little family that ever walked the earth. In 2012, when I was hugely pregnant, I graduated from Hamline University with a master's of writing for children; three weeks later, I had a son. It was quite a time.

My first book, **Courageous Women of the Civil War: Soldiers, Spies, Medics, and More** was published by Chicago Review Press in August 2016. This is a series of profiles of women who fought or cared for the wounded during the Civil War.

I've been sending novels out to publishers and agents since 1995, and have racked up I don't know how many hundreds of rejections. I kept getting very close – but not close enough. Agents kept saying, "You're a very good writer, you have an excellent grasp of craft, but I just don't feel that 'spark'...." Even after *Courageous Women* was published, they still weren't interested in my books.

In September 2016, I rage-quit traditional publishing and started self-publishing, because I wanted to get my books out to people who *would* feel that 'spark.' In my first year, I published 15 books. This year I plan to repeat that. (When you've been writing novels for over 20 years, you're going to have a bit of a backlog.) I am working my way completely through it and having a complete blast. I love doing cover work and designing the book interiors. I work full-time as a proofreader, so I handle that in my books as well.

And now I'm finding fans of my books who do feel that 'spark.' They're peaches, every one of them.

I'm finally doing what I was put on this earth to do.

There's no better feeling than that.

If you like this book, please leave a review on my BookBub or Goodreads page. Reviews help me get more readers.

Thanks so much for reading!
melindacordell.com

Subscribe to my newsletter
and get a free gardening book:
https://www.subscribepage.com/garden

www.ingramcontent.com/pod-product-compliance
Lightning Source LLC
Chambersburg PA
CBHW022101020426
42335CB00012B/781